PG-99
PG 66
PG 65
PG 47
PG 34
PG 27
PG 22

CONTENTS

FOREWORD

The Treaty of Rome of 1957 described the goal of European integration as the ever closer union between the peoples of Europe. The Treaty of Maastricht, agreed in December 1991, marks a new phase in that process by establishing a European Union. It deserves the closest examination by the Irish public, particularly as it will be the subject of a referendum.

The Institute of European Affairs, which was established in 1990 as an independent forum to provide objective analysis of the integration process, has published this analysis of the Treaty as a contribution to informed public debate within Ireland on the meaning and implications of this first phase of European Union.

It consists of commentaries on the Treaty's main themes and provisions by a group of experts drawn from a wide field of disciplines. The views expressed in this volume are those of the individual authors and do not necessarily represent the opinion of the Institute. They can be taken, individually and collectively as an objective examination of a Treaty which could prove of long term significance to this country and to the future of Europe. This volume should be read in conjunction with the two separate studies on Political Union and on Economic and Monetary Union published by the Institute in 1991. These provide both the background and the context in which to assess this publication, which like the Maastricht Treaty itself covers both of these related subjects.

In preparing the various papers published in this volume, the authors had the benefit of advice from a the working group of which I was Chairperson. I wish to thank its members for the time they devoted to this task and for their contributions which were of such assistance to the team of authors. On a personal note, I wish to record my appreciation of the expertise and energy which Professor Patrick Keatinge brought to his role as editor of this book. His contribution as editor and author was invaluable.

James Dooge,
Chairperson of the Working Group.

INTRODUCTION

The Treaty on European Union, or Treaty of Maastricht as it is generally known, is an important but long and complex legal text. It builds on foundations laid down in previous Treaties, agreed and implemented over the last forty years; like them it is the work of many hands guided by different cultures. It contains amendments and innovations of varying significance, couched in the technical language of the legal draftsman, which inevitably makes it difficult to grasp just what is at stake. The purpose of this book is to try to analyse the Treaty in a way that is intelligible and relevant to the general reader, and to highlight the implications for Ireland.

Before entering this maze, in Part One we place the Treaty of Maastricht in its historical context, tracing the evolution of European integration up to the agreement reached in the Dutch town in December 1991. We argue that this evolution, and the possibility of its continuation in the future, can be understood at a general level in terms of the aspiration to create a federal union.

In Part Two we examine the political processes of the new Union. Chapter 2, on the structure of the Treaty, reveals an important distinction between three main types of activity – the so-called 'pillars'. The first is composed of the amended Community Treaties, under the supranational system of decision-making and subject to judicial review by the European Court of Justice. The other two pillars are dealt with in the conventional 'intergovernmental' way, based on unanimous agreement between national governments, outside the jurisdiction of the Court. This continues the hybrid system of policymaking, already employed in the Single European Act.

The Treaty contains a number of institutional innovations which raise questions about the effectiveness of decision-making and which are discussed in Chapter 3. The changes also include a definition of citizenship and new procedures for the European Parliament, and in Chapter 4 we ask whether these reforms make the policymakers more accountable to the people they serve. The increasing complexity of the policy process, operating at both the European and national levels, can all too easily lead to a democratic deficit.

Part Three summarises the changes in policies in the Community pillar. The extent to which the policy scope of the Community has been extended into new policy areas is described in Chapter 5. The commitment to an Economic and Monetary Union takes pride of place and is analysed in detail in Chapter 6. Although there is provision for movement towards a single currency, the Treaty falls short of a full EMU. From Ireland's point of view the consolidation of economic and social cohesion was a major goal in the negotiations leading to Maastricht, and the result is assessed in Chapter 7. Ultimately, the significance of cohesion depends on the future evolution of the political process, though at least the Treaty commitments may be used as a lever to develop redistributive policies. Finally, the ambiguous outcome of the controversial negotiations on Social Policy is explored in Chapter 8.

The two intergovernmental pillars are explained in Part Four. The most substantial of these is the Common Foreign and Security Policy, which is the subject of Chapter 9. Based on the established process of foreign policy cooperation, it includes a tentative experiment with majority voting and, from an Irish point of view, a controversial reference to an eventual defence policy. Although this does not require an immediate change to the stance of military neutrality, it does raise basic questions about the state's involvement in the post-Cold War world. The other intergovernmental pillar, dealing with Cooperation in Justice and Home Affairs, comes into Treaty form for the first time and is described in Chapter 10.

The Treaty on European Union was not conceived as the final stage in European integration, and the prospects for Europe after Maastricht are explored in Part Five. In Chapter 11 we pose the question whether the effects of increased membership will not of itself lead to further important changes. The probable enlargement to a Union of about twenty states within the next decade does not simply amount to 'more of the same'; it may lead to a qualitative change in the way integration is organised. In Chapter 12 we ask whether, and to what extent, the Treaty is moving towards a full federal union. Both in form and content the Union it creates contains a mixture of federal and intergovernmental elements. However, we conclude that it is not yet on the threshold of federal union, but rather is an increasingly complex confederation.

Part Six explores the relationship between the Treaty and the Irish Constitution. Chapter 13 deals with the necessity for a referendum, the legal consequences of non-ratification, and the question of whether a further referendum will be required following any future change which might affect Irish neutrality. The Protocol originally inserted to protect the Irish constitutional ban on abortion is examined in Chapter 14, in the wake of the controversy following the Supreme Court judgement on the case of X versus the Attorney General.

Finally, in Part Seven, we focus on the referendum on the ratification of the Treaty. Chapter 15 summaries the issues and suggests that the Treaty faces the Irish people with serious choices about their political and economic future. The principal options facing the voters are then laid out in Chapter 16 which concludes that their response will be the most important political decision of this generation.

Acknowledgements

The authors of this study owe a considerable debt to the members of a round-table discussion group established by the Institute of European Affairs, who discussed earlier drafts of the individual chapters. A similar contribution was made by the Institute's membership in Brussels, and by several individuals who provided detailed comments. Their comments were much appreciated, though, of course, the responsibility for errors of fact and for views expressed is entirely that of the authors.

In facing a very tight schedule we were also assisted by the prompt provision of documentation by the information services of the EC Commission and the European Parliament. Finally, our thanks are due to the publications committee of the Institute, chaired by Iain MacAulay, and assisted by Odran Reid, Jean Barker, Victor McBrien and Dominic O'Toole. All concerned showed great patience in bringing this book to publication with the least delay after the signing of the Treaty of Maastricht.

Patrick Keatinge,
Editor.
April 1992.

THE CONTEXT

1. FROM COMMUNITY TO UNION

Patrick Keatinge

In the early hours of 11 December 1991, the leaders of the twelve member states of the European Community, meeting in Maastricht in the Netherlands, agreed the text of a Treaty on European Union. After twelve months work in two parallel Inter Governmental Conferences on Economic and Monetary Union (EMU) and Political Union, this agreement marked "a new stage in the process of creating an ever closer Union among the peoples of Europe" (Common Provisions A). Before identifying just what is new in the Treaty, and assessing its significance for the member states, it is necessary to place this event in a broader context. First, we see how the Treaty of Maastricht fits into the historical evolution of European integration. Second, we look more closely at a recurrent theme in that historical record, the aspiration to create a *federal* union. This helps us understand what 'ever closer Union' means now, and what it might come to mean in the future.

Unions In History

Political union is an ambiguous term, and has been attached to many different historical realities. In the Irish context it recalls the *involuntary* union between Ireland and Great Britain. Although the Act of Union created an uneasy association of nations, there was no union of equal states; the relationship was marked by the domination of the larger entity without any significant autonomy for the smaller.

Even in modern cases where individual states exist within a union, the legal form may be less important than the overwhelming domination of a central authority. It was the Communist Party of the Soviet Union, often relying on arbitrary coercion, which held the USSR together between

1917 and 1991. Similarly, it was a communist party which provided the cement of the Yugoslav federation, with the ironic twist that the authority of Yugoslav communism derived much of its strength from the threat of the Soviet Union. The collapse of both these unions provided a dramatic contrast to the negotiations on European Union, but hardly represented a rebuttal of what the negotiators were trying to achieve.

It is more appropriate to consider Maastricht in the context of *voluntary* unions of states. The case that usually comes to mind is the United States of America, but although its form of government provides an important point of reference, the USA today is a fully-fledged federal state which has clearly moved beyond the point at which the EC states are at present. The European Community has been more akin to a treaty-based association of more or less autonomous but interdependent states – in short, a *confederation.*

Confederations often appear in the historical writings of the English-speaking world as an awkward stage, like adolescence, on the way to political maturity. With the American experience in mind, they are justified mainly as stepping stones to the creation of a single state, whether federal or unitary in form. However, although the American Confederation had a very brief life(1781-1789), it can be argued that aspects of its federal persona were not fully accepted until after the civil war in the 1860s.

In European history, on the other hand, confederations have some-times proved to be rather more durable. The Swiss Confederation lasted from 1291 to 1848 (with time out for a Napoleonic interlude); only then did it become in effect a single federal state, though it is still described as a confederation. A Dutch confederation existed between 1579 and 1795, subsequently becoming a unitary state. Another EC state, Germany, had a complex experience of confederal union, in the German Bund of 1815-1866, before eventually becoming a single federal state which is a model of its kind.

Confederations are generally based on freely-negotiated treaties between separate political units; however, the treaties may go beyond normal inter-state agreements in attempting to give the respective unions some capacity to make law for their members. Historically, the major motivation behind their creation was to provide for their members' defence, and more generally, their security. With the increase in inter-national trade following the industrial revolution, a concern with the 'general welfare' led to the more elaborate forms of economic union with which we are familiar today.

European Integration

Both sources of motivation can be seen in the development of integration in Western Europe after World War II. Jean Monnet's strategy of "concrete, resolute action on a limited but decisive point" found its first expression in the European Coal and Steel Community (ECSC), which established common control over the economic basis of French and German military potential. This 'community' can be seen as a partial union, designed as much as a means to peace between Germany and her former enemies as it was for material welfare. Economic objectives were more pronounced in subsequent developments in the 1950s, with the Treaties of Rome on the European Economic Community(EEC) and Euratom, but the security rationale for West European integration never disappeared altogether.

The major positive moves in the 1960s, however, were economic – the establishment of a customs union, the EEC's role in world trade negotiations, and the creation of a Common Agricultural Policy (CAP). The latter was a particular incentive for Ireland in considering its relationship with the emerging Community, though twelve years were to elapse between the decision to apply for membership and its achievement in 1973. The long-term political consequences of membership were not elaborated in any detail in the original treaties, but the applicant countries were reminded by the Commission that they were "not only joining an economic and social undertaking, but that they will be required to participate fully in creating a continent which is economically and politically united".

During the greater part of Ireland's membership of the European Community this objective has seemed remote. In any case, Ireland's detachment from the 'foundation trauma' of European integration – World War II – has done little to encourage appreciation of this political motivation. In the period following our accession, the 'continent' remained sharply divided on Cold War lines, and the economic challenges of the 1970s and early 1980s (oil shocks, stagflation and unemployment) were more acute than in the 1960s. The enlargement of the EC was difficult, especially the absorption of a United Kingdom which was ambivalent towards its links in Europe.

Against such a negative background, the capacity of the Community increased piecemeal. Policy development included the creation of a Regional Fund, the expansion of the Social Fund, and in 1979 the European Monetary System (EMS). Institutional changes included European

Political Cooperation (EPC), for foreign policy consultation, the regular involvement of government leaders in the European Council, and direct elections to the European Parliament.

The untidiness of the EC's institutions was matched by an increasing unevenness in the commitments undertaken by the member states. This phenomenon – sometimes known as 'variable geometry' – involves different transitional arrangements, and the possibility of some states opting out of specific activities. The prospect of a more or less permanent 'two-tier' or 'two-speed' form of integration, in which the poorer parts of the Community would find it even more difficult to catch up with the rest, was reflected in the pessimism of this period.

Two Roads To Maastricht

However, the mid-1980s saw a revival in confidence. The commitment to complete the Single Market by the end of 1992 re-established the focus on the core of economic integration, and the Single European Act (SEA) provided another 'limited but decisive' institutional reform. In Ireland the ratification of the SEA was controversial, the Supreme Court ruling in the Crotty case that the changes were such to require a referendum. One element in this ruling concerned the legal codification of the existing process of European Political Cooperation, the significance of which was interpreted in quite different ways by the five judges. A confused referendum campaign resulted in approval of the new treaty by a two to one majority, but with a low turnout of 44 per cent.

Nevertheless, the implementation of the SEA in 1987 was accompanied by a new degree of political will in the Community as a whole. This was demonstrated in the achievement of stability in the EC budget in 1988, allowing for a substantial increase in the Structural Funds, the main instrument of the principle of 'cohesion' by which economic disparities were to be reduced. The following year the Delors Report on Economic and Monetary Union was accepted, thus paving the way for an Inter Governmental Conference on EMU. The path of an economic logic in which a single currency was seen as the corollary of a single market provided the obvious route to further integration. Although the British government did not share that view, it appealed both to the Germans, as leaders of the European economy, and to the French, for whom integration has been seen as the best means of influencing their largest neighbour. More generally, the revival of the goal of EMU was a sign that the Community was being taken more seriously by its members.

It was also being taken more seriously by the outside world. Since 1989 the dramatic and fundamental changes in world politics have provided an additional source of demands for further integration. The 'continent' of Europe has been transformed by the end of the Cold War, followed by the dissolution of the Eastern bloc, one member of which has already been absorbed into the EC through the unification of Germany. The predominance of Germany – and the corresponding apprehensions of the French and British governments – was suddenly enhanced; for those who interpret integration as a sophisticated form of balance of power politics, the balance which had been so long taken for granted was now threatened. The decision to hold an Inter Governmental Conference on Political Union, alongside that on EMU, was taken in this context, at a special meeting of the European Council in Dublin in April 1990.

Both Inter Governmental Conferences were formally launched at the European Council in Rome in December 1990, and proceeded in parallel throughout the following year. During this period the economic background deteriorated, with a general recession and the immediate costs of German unification leading to a nervousness both inside Germany and among her partners. Political instability continued outside the Community; war in the Gulf was followed by civil war in Yugoslavia and the collapse of the Soviet Union. The negotiations were conducted by senior civil servants, with regular interventions by government ministers and with reference to the 'summit meeting' at the European Council in Luxembourg in June. As is the case with any international agreement, the negotiations were conducted on the basis of confidentiality, though given their protracted nature and the number of states involved it was possible to identify the main issues and national attitudes from quite an early stage.

That is not to say that the precise outcome could have been predicted before the final top-level meeting at Maastricht in December. Like every treaty associated with European integration, the Treaty is based on a complex compromise between the signatories. Broadly, they might be categorised as 'maximalists' or 'minimalists' with regard to the desirability of the extent and pace of integration, though this distinction does not do justice to the dilemmas which each government faced in identifying its own bottom line in the final package. The provisions on Economic and Monetary Union were cast in a German mould, but Germany did not achieve its aims so far as the European Parliament was concerned. The British government entered the negotiations as the leading minimalist, and succeeded in 'opting out' of commitments to the EMU and Social

Policy; it did not prevent these policies being developed in a Union which itself was committed to further development. Nor did it prevent a consolidation of cohesion, which was pressed by the poor states, including Ireland. France entered the negotiations as advocates of the immediate establishment of a fully-fledged European defence system, but NATO – still under American leadership – remains the key organisation in this field.

Nowhere is compromise more obvious than in the structure of the Treaty. Like the Single European Act, it includes two different types of decision-making. The truly integrationist form of 'supranational decision-making', with its emphasis on majority voting, is found in the Community pillar, covering economic and social policy. The much less constraining 'intergovernmental' form, in which unanimity is the norm, is retained in the other two pillars, dealing with foreign and security policy and justice and home affairs. For the Commission, and several member states, this particular compromise is seen as an unsatisfactory interim measure. In this view, the 'ever closer Union' should go beyond an untidy confederal compromise to create a truly federal union.

The Measure Of Maastricht

The ambition to transform the separate states of Europe not merely into a confederation but into a single federal entity – a United States of Europe – has been a feature on the landscape of European politics since the catastrophe of World War II. It can be seen today in the vision and rhetoric of significant political leaders and organisations, as well as in the institutional arrangements of the European Community. However, the fact that it is still not universally shared is equally obvious, and may be in part attributed to the different historical experiences among the member states. Thus Germans, with over forty years experience of a successful federal system, find the British obsession with a centralised unitary state hard to understand.

Yet although the federal idea remains controversial, it can nevertheless serve as an indicator of where any particular confederal reality lies in the process of integration. By identifying both the policies and institutions characteristically found in a federal *state* it is possible to establish an overall yardstick against which the Treaty of Maastricht can be measured. This in turn may clarify the context of the debate on the desirability of further integration.

Federal states reflect the desire to allow for considerable diversity in their society by organising government on distinct levels, with different tasks being undertaken by the central (federal) government and the governments of the individual states. Although there is considerable variation in the ways in which established federal states apply the principle, the following *policies* are typically seen as the responsibility of the federal government:

– a customs union, with a common external tariff and commercial policy

– free movement of all factors of production

– a federal budget, based on the taxation power of the central government, usually sufficient to allow for redistributive policies throughout the union

– monetary policy, including a single currency

– foreign and security policy, including the defence of the union against external threats.

Following the principle of 'subsidiarity', i.e. that authority should be exercised at the lowest effective level, the individual states are responsible for what may be regarded as their domestic affairs.

The policy *processes* and institutions of a federal state, like those of a democratic unitary state, are based on the rule of law and representative organs, but with a particular emphasis on these features:

– an explicit separation of powers between the individual states and the union, guaranteed in a constitution which cannot be easily amended

– a highly developed process of judicial review

– a bicameral legislature, to allow for representation of the individual states as such, as well as representation on the basis of the popular vote.

Will the Treaty of Maastricht move the states in the new European Union closer to this federal model? Does it even merit the appellation of 'union'? In recent years advocates of a federal Europe have reserved this term for a very advanced form of confederation, so advanced as to be *on the threshold* of transformation into a federal state. This approach, most fully developed in the European Parliament's Draft Treaty of 1984, provides a rather less ambitious benchmark for an assessment of Maastricht. In *policy* terms, such a European Union would involve a significant, and increasing, role for the Union in tasks generally undertaken by federal states, though perhaps without the central control of armed forces. In terms of *process,* majority voting among member states would be the general rule in decision-making; the Council in which they were represented would become in effect the second chamber of a bicameral legislature alongside the directly-elected European Parliament.

The Range Of Possibilities

It is argued in Chapter 12, that, although it encompasses several significant changes, the Treaty of Maastricht cannot yet be placed on the threshold of a federal state. Nor is there any guarantee that it will be. It is not inconceivable that the Union thereby created will remain as a confederation, perhaps adopting a form without any clear historical precedent. Indeed, while the Treaty contains elements which have a very strong federal character, such as the projected single currency, these sit alongside others which fall far short of that mark. The policy process is if anything a more confusing mixture of federal and intergovernmental ideas; the nominal inclusion of defence does not even go as far as the guarantee of mutual assistance typical of a conventional alliance.

Any new agreement such as that made at Maastricht can only provide a framework for the future; the force of events both inside and outside the Union will also contribute to the direction it takes. Nevertheless, the choice of a constitutional framework – for that is what the Treaty amounts to – is always an important act of political faith. Moreover, it is a choice which all the member states, and in Ireland's case its people, are now required to make. The Treaty of Maastricht is thus a basic document in Irish politics.

THE UNION PROCESSES

2. THE TREATY: STRUCTURE AND THEMES

Brigid Laffan

The Treaty heralds a qualitative change in the goals and scope of European integration and includes significant alterations to the Community's policy process. It is lengthy and much more complex than previous Treaties. In this chapter, we outline the structure of the Treaty and discuss its main themes.

Structure Of The Treaty

The Treaty establishes a European Union. The Union consists of three areas of activity; held together by common provisions at the beginning and final provisions at the end. The three areas of activity are:

- the European Community (Paris and Rome Treaties as extended by the Single Act and the Maastricht Treaty)

- cooperation on foreign and security policy (Title V: Article J)

- cooperation on judicial and home affairs (Title V1: Article K).

The Union may be described as consisting of three pillars. Thus the European Community is incorporated into the Union as one of three pillars or strands. The three pillars do not just connote three arenas of policy cooperation but also lead to different models of policymaking in the Union. Put simply, there is a major distinction in the Union between policymaking based on the Community method (EEC Treaty format), on the one hand, and intergovernmental cooperation, on the other.

The Community method involves a complex interaction between institutions representing the interests of the member states and those with a supranational character. By supranational is meant institutions which are in principle independent of the member states and national governments. The European Council and the Council of Ministers are the main intergovernmental fora in the Community. The Commission, the Parliament and the European Court of Justice are supranational in character.

Provisions on foreign and security policy and on cooperation in judicial matters are characterised largely by intergovernmental cooperation in the Treaty. National governments are intent on maintaining control over the development of these two areas because they impinge on core areas of state activity. There is a much greater sharing of sovereignty in the Community pillar than in either of the other two and the quasi-federal character of the Institutions is much stronger.

There was considerable contention during the negotiations on the 'three pillars'. The imagery used to illustrate the choice facing the negotiators was that of a tree or a temple. A tree had connotations of a coherent framework, a single centre of decision-making and policies branching out from the core or trunk. The alternative image was that of a Greek temple with separate columns. The Commission and those states pursuing a 'maximalist' outcome from the negotiations argued in favour of a Treaty based on 'unicity', Euro-parlance for a Treaty based on the Community method of policymaking. This proved impossible at the negotiating table given the sensitive nature of foreign policy and judicial cooperation and these were placed in their own separate decision-making systems. Consequently, three different pillars emerged which, when joined together by the common and final provisions, constitute the new European Union.

The three pillars, which represent the temple, allow the member states to reach agreements on areas of policy that are traditionally associated with national sovereignty. Experience of dealing with these issues in an intergovernmental framework may in time lead to the adoption of the Community method. European integration, involving as it does voluntary agreements among states, is unlikely to proceed on the basis of a uniform model. While this can lead to an absence of coherence and give rise to complex institutional arrangements, it allows the member states to widen the scope of their common concerns and common rule-making.

The Treaty is a conglomeration of amendments to existing Treaties and a codification of cooperation that did not previously have a legal basis. In addition to the main text of the Treaty, there are seventeen protocols clarifying or elaborating on the text and on the application of the Treaty to certain policy issues or member states. Protocols serve to establish the framework for the implementation of the Treaty to take account of special circumstances in the member states. Protocols are legally binding and allow for specific derogations from the Treaty. A protocol may also specify how the Treaty will be applied or interpreted in particular areas.

For example, Irish policymakers negotiated a special protocol saying that nothing in the Treaty of Maastricht or other EC treaties affects the application in Ireland of Article 40.3.3 of the Irish constitution dealing with the right to life of the unborn. This protocol was included in the Treaty at the request of the Irish government. Following the judgement of the European Court of Justice in the case of Grogan v SPUC on the right to information about abortion services in Britain, the Government felt it necessary to underpin the Constitutional provision on the rights of the unborn with a special protocol. The legal and constitutional implications of the protocol are dealt with by Hogan and Hyland (in Chapter 13). There are some thirteen declarations on various aspects of the Treaty by the Conference acting as one or the member states. Such declarations, unlike protocols, have no legal status but are statements of political intent (see Tables 1-3 for a synopsis of the Treaty of Maastricht).

The Treaty is further complicated by its provisions on social policy. The member states, with the exception of the United Kingdom, reached an agreement on the implementation of the 1989 Social Charter outside the strict confines of the Union Treaties but on the basis of existing EC policy in the social domain. Deep-rooted conflict concerning social policy lead to the extraordinary device of including the new chapter on social policy as a protocol signed by eleven of the twelve states because the UK was unwilling to accept a new chapter on social policy in the main body of the Treaty.

The political, legal and economic effects of the social policy decision are as yet unclear. In effect, the eleven have agreed to expand the remit of social policy and to adapt the decision-making rules but their intention is to act within the EC's institutional system. Hence the stipulation in the protocol that the eleven may have "recourse to the institutions, procedures and mechanisms of the EC". The existing social policy articles of the Rome Treaty and the Single Act will continue to operate in areas that fall within the scope of these two Treaties. The eleven will then attempt to go beyond this among themselves. 'Variable geometry', a term used to describe cooperation among a limited group of states, is now a feature of this policy area.

General Themes Of The Treaty

The common provisions of the Treaty are significant because they establish the general principles that govern the Treaty. Article A specifies that the "High Contracting Parties" establish a European Union. The earlier Single Act simply included an aspiration to "transform relations as a whole among their States into a European Union". Dispute about the essence of what they were trying to achieve led to the substitution of a strong statement about a "Union with a federal goal" with a rather more ambiguous statement referring to an "ever closer Union among the peoples of Europe".

The latter can be found in the original Rome Treaty. The UK was unwilling to include a reference to a 'federal goal' in the Treaty given its general antipathy towards supranational institutions. This is unfortunate in many respects because the use of the word 'federal' would have clarified the kind of polity and political institutions the drafters of the Treaty were aiming for.

Paradoxically, although the federal goal of the Treaty is not acknowledged, 'subsidiarity', a federalist principle has a central place in the Treaty. 'Subsidiarity' is usually taken to mean that decisions in a political system should be taken at the lowest effective or feasible level. It is intended as a counter-weight to a centralisation of decision-making within the Union. European integration has sometimes been portrayed as an inexorable process leading to greater and greater powers at the centre.

'Subsidiarity' places limits on the Community's policy reach. The need for subsidiarity stems from the political, cultural and economic diversity in Europe. Article F says that "The Union shall respect the national identities of its Member States". The common provisions suggest that within the Union "decisions are taken as closely as possible to the citizens" (Article A). This raises the question not just about the relationship between the Union and national governments but also the distribution of power within states. European integration has often been described as a process leading to a flow of power from central governments upwards to the Community and downwards to regions. A 'Europe of regions' is frequently cited as one of the benefits of integration. While a 'Europe of the regions' will not replace a Europe of states, given the pivotal role of national governments both within states and in the Community, the Treaty acknowledges the role of regions in the Union by establishing a Committee of the Regions. This development stems from a recognition of the growth of regionalism in many states in Western Europe. Moreover, it is an acknowledgment that EC politics and policies are beginning to bite into the policy competences of regional governments, notably the German Lander.

Article B of the Treaty stipulates that "The Union shall respect the principle of subsidiarity". This is an attempt to ensure that in areas of shared competence, the Community does not amass an ever-widening range of responsibilities. Subsidiarity, as a principle, can be seen in the treaty articles on EMU, education, and culture, for example. Article 3b contains some guidelines for translating the goal of 'subsidiarity' into the day to day politics of the Community. First, it mentions the "scale or effects of proposed action". In other words, the Community should only engage in action when a policy area or a problem can only be tackled in a wider context than that of the member states. Second, it specifies that the "community shall not go beyond what is necessary to achieve the objectives of the Treaty".

The clause on subsidiarity will have both political and legal consequences. From now on, the Commission will have to make a good case when it proposes to widen the scope of Community involvement in a policy area. A member state or institution will be able to test issues using this principle in the European Court of Justice. The Court is likely to have to elaborate on the legal implications of the principle in the 1990s. Notwithstanding this, there will continue to be conflict between the Community and national levels and among the member states about the appropriate location of policy responsibility. 'Subsidiarity' could well become a political weapon in the bargaining process.

Sovereignty

The Treaty of Maastricht, like its precursors, has implications for the exercise of national sovereignty. Because of the far-reaching goal of EMU and the acceleration of integration in other fields, the Treaty represents a significant transfer of powers to the Union. Its implementation will have a major impact on the conduct of many areas of public policy and on the political institutions of the twelve member states. The twelve have agreed to jointly limit their legal sovereignty within the terms of the Treaty. The voluntary acceptance and promotion of a further pooling of formal sovereignty owes much to the challenges facing West European states at the beginning of the 1990s. For many states, a pooling of sovereignty is preferable to legal autonomy without the political power to exercise it.

An acceleration of economic integration is a follow-on from the commitment to the Single Market in the Single Act. A renewed emphasis on Political Union stems from the challenge of German unification, the collapse of communism and the end of an international system dominated by two superpowers. Even Western Europe's larger states feel the need to deepen integration to meet these challenges. That said, all of the member states are cautious about sharing competence in sensitive areas of policy, notably foreign policy and judicial cooperation.

There is a tension between further integration and national sovereignty. Concern for where decisions will be made, and the desire to influence decisions that affect daily lives is part of the debate on sovereignty. Fear that a deepening of integration may mean a further diminution in governments capacity to mediate with economic and social forces sharpens the debate on sovereignty. Attachment to the symbols of legal sovereignty is perhaps more evident in some member states than others. Yet for all states there are sensitive areas that for one reason or another are core political values.

The Treaty of Maastricht is an effort to match the political framework to economic realities and to deal with the revolution in world politics. It marks a further change in the exercise of national sovereignty and points to a further pooling of sovereignty by the turn of the century. For smaller states, strong EC institutions are a better guarantee that their interests will be heard than a system dominated by the larger and more powerful states. Thus Maastricht, while it marks a further pooling of Ireland's legal sovereignty, affords this small state access to the negotiating arena where Europe's future will be determined. Ireland's ability to influence decisions will depend very much on the capacity of its governmental system to work out a strategic approach to integration and to win allies in the perpetual negotiations that characterise the Community.

Table I
Treaty of Maastricht

Common Provisions

Six Articles on the objectives of the Union, the European Council, the coherence of its institutional framework, subsidiarity, and fundamental rights. These articles cover the three pillars of the Union.

Provisions Amending the EEC Treaty: Pillar I

Principles

Eight Articles,tasks of the EC, policy scope, subsidiarity, institutions.

Citizenship of the Union

Six Articles, freedom of movement, political rights and consular services.

Community Policies

Amendments to a range of Articles dealing with existing policy

Inclusion of new policy areas

– EMU Treaty Articles
– Trans-European Networks
– Industry
– Public Health
– Culture
– Development cooperation
– Consumer protection.

Association of overseas territories

Institutions

General Provisions

Provisions Amending the ECSC Treaty:Pillar I

Provisions Amending the EURATOM Treaty: Pillar I

Provisions on a Common Foreign and Security Policy:Pillar II

Provisions on Cooperation in the fields of Justice and Home Affairs: Pillar III

Final Provisions

Protocols

Declarations.

Table II

List of Protocols to the Treaty of Maastricht

Political Union

Protocol on Economic and Social Cohesion

Protocol on Social Policy and Agreement concluded between the Member States of the European Community with the exception of the UK

Protocol on the Acquisition of Property in Denmark

Protocol on Article 119 of EEC Treaty (Social Security)

Protocol on the Economic and Social Committee and the Committee of the Regions

Protocol Annexed to the Treaty on the European Union and the Treaties Establishing the European Communities (Nothing in these treaties shall affect the application in Ireland of Article 40.3.3 of the Constitution of Ireland).

Economic and Monetary Union

Protocol on the excessive deficit procedure

Protocol on the Statute of the EMI

Protocol on the Statute of the ESCB/ECB

Protocol on the convergence criteria of the transition to the third stage

Protocol on the privileges and immunities of the ECB and the EMI

Protocol on Denmark

Protocol on Portugal

Protocol on the transition to the third stage

Protocol on certain provisions relating to the UK

Protocol on certain provisions relating to Denmark

Protocol on France.

Table III

Declarations attached to the Treaty of Maastricht

Political Union

Declaration on the Role of National Parliaments in the European Union

Declaration on the Conference of the Parliaments

Declaration on the Right of Access to Information

Declaration on Estimated Costs under Commission Proposals

Declaration on the Implementation of Community Law

Declaration on Assessment of the Environmental Impact of Community Measures

Declaration on the Court of Auditors

Declaration on cooperation with Charitable Associations

Declaration on the Protection of Animals

Declaration on Title XI of the EEC Treaty(nature conservation)

Declaration on the representation of the interests of overseas countries and territories

Declaration on the Overseas Departments and outermost regions

Declaration by the European Council on areas which could be the subject of joint action

A number of separate declarations are appended to individual Treaty articles in the text of the Treaty.

Economic and Monetary Union

Declaration on Title III and VI of EEC Treaty

Declaration on Title VI of EC Treaty

Declaration on monetary cooperation with non-Community countries

Declaration on monetary relations with San Marino, Vatican City and Monaco

Declaration on Article 73.

TREATY OF MAASTRICHT

THE TEMPLE

Pillar I	Pillar II	Pillar III
Amendments to EC Treaties	Common Foreign and Security Policy	Judicial Cooperation
Subsidiarity	Objectives	Scope
Enhancement of some policy areas	Decision-making	Decision-making
Institutional changes	Scope	
EP powers	Relations with WEU	
Appointment of Commission	1996 Review	
Committee of the Regions		
Economic and Monetary Union		

3. THE NEW INSTITUTIONAL FRAMEWORK

Brigid Laffan

The Treaty of Maastricht changes not only what the EC does but how it goes about the business of arriving at policy stances and legally-binding decisions. The Treaty includes a series of changes to the role and function of the main institutions. This affects the working of each institution and their relationship. Two questions must be asked, first, do these changes improve the effectiveness of the Community's policy process. Second, do they make them more democratic. Concern for accountability and transparency has been a major issue on the Community's agenda for many years. If the Union is to become more important in all our lives, then there must be control over the activities of its institutions. Individual citizens must feel that the decisions coming from Brussels are legitimate and taken by accountable politicians. The Union must strive to be both effective and democratic. The main institutional changes are continued in this chapter and are then assessed in the following chapter as to whether or not Maastricht improves the effectiveness of the Community's policy process.

The Main Institutional Changes

The Council System The European Council has assumed a pivotal role in the development of the Community since its establishment in 1975, outside the strict confines of the Treaty. This is confirmed in the Treaty of Maastricht which specifies that the "European Council shall provide the Union with the necessary impetus for its development and shall define the general political guidelines thereof" (Article D, Common Provisions). This role of strategic goal-setting and political leadership is reinforced in the chapter on the CFSP which gives the European Council the responsibility for establishing 'general guidelines' (Article CFSP).

The European Council shares this role with the Commission which retains a key role in drafting legislation and in establishing the broad outline of the 'general interest of the Community'. The role of the European Council is less apparent in the third pillar on judicial cooperation.

The European Council brings the political authority of the national political leaders to bear on the politics of the Union. In a political system that lacks an identifiable centre of political power and authority, i.e., a government, this is a central ingredient for effectiveness. The extension of qualified majority voting to new areas of policy will serve to speed up decision-making in those areas and will reinforce the behavioural changes that the Single Act engendered in the Council.

The Parliament Since 1979, the Parliament has sought to strengthen its role in the Community's policy process by stressing its democratic credentials. After Maastricht, the powers of the Parliament are now exercised through five distinct procedures. These are: 1. Co-Decision; 2. Cooperation; 3. Assent; 4. Consultation; and 5. The Budget. The Treaty establishes a new procedure (189 B co-decision) in a number of policy areas. It extends the use of the cooperation procedure (189 c), established by the Single Act, to new areas of policy and also extends the assent procedure. It is impossible to predict what the impact of the new procedures on the efficiency and effectiveness of the Community's institutions.

Clearly the new co-decision procedure, which makes provision for a process of conciliation between the Council and the Parliament, will lengthen the legislative process although there are time limits (six weeks) contained in the Treaty for this part of the process. Given that such a conciliation process comes at the end of a lengthy dialogue involving the Council, the Parliament and the Commission, there is an inbuilt bias in favour of agreement. Moreover, the Council may adopt the text even if it fails to reach agreement with the Parliament, unless the Parliament rejects the text by an absolute majority of its members within six weeks. The Parliament could not resort to this action frequently because the long tortuous process of fashioning agreement would have to begin again. The existence of three different legislative procedures and a separate budgetary procedure serves to increase the complexity of the policy process.

The Treaty grants the Parliament a role in the appointment of the Commission which will have an impact on the effectiveness of the policy process and on political accountability over time. From 1995 onwards, the life of a Commission will be coterminous with that of the Parliament. In the three months after each direct election, the Parliament will be consulted on the appointment of the President of the Commission and will have a vote on the Commission as a whole. This will lend coherence to the Community's political system and will strengthen the relationship between the representative and executive branches. The Commission will have to pay more attention to the wishes of the Parliament and may see it as a source of policy ideas.

The assent procedure has been extended to cover new kinds of agreements, notably, international agreements, a uniform electoral system, citizenship, rules governing the Structural Funds, and amendments to the protocol dealing with the European system of central banks. The right to set up committees of enquiry and to receive petitions is recognised in the Treaty and the Parliament may appoint an Ombudsman.

The Commission   The Commission has been granted a right of initiative in relation to the Common Foreign and Security Policy. Although this is not a sole right of initiative it highlights the Commission's growing importance in this field. Moreover, the Commission's right of initiative in the committee system has been more or less protected, although the provision in Article 189b for a conciliation process gives the Parliament some autonomy from the Commission in the legislative process.

Potentially one of the most significant changes is the commitment to examine the Commission's size; if agreement can be reached, the larger states will no longer have a right to two Commissioners. From 1995 onwards, the term of office of a Commissioner is to increase from four to five years so that the duration of a Commission matches that of the Parliament.

Committee of the Regions   The Treaty establishes for the first time a body responsible for representing the regional and local authorities in the Community. The Committee is modelled on the Economic and Social Committee with 189 members. Its members are appointed by the Council for a period of four years on the basis of proposals from the member states. The Committee has no more than an advisory role in the legislative process and its members are not instructed delegates. Its role will depend very much on how it evolves and whether or not it can become the focus for regional authorities in the Community.

Effective Decision-Making?

The Community's institutions and its political system face a major challenge when translating the ambitious goals of a single currency and an expanded range of policies into reality. The success of the Single Act lay in the impetus it gave to decision-making in the Community characterised by an increased use of majority voting and a strengthening of the Parliament's role in the policy process. The Treaty of Maastricht contains no such clearcut relationship between policy goals and institutional provisions. In fact, it has added greatly to the complexity of the Community's decision-making process.

The institutional changes introduced by the Treaty are characteristic of the incremental approach to reform which dominates the Community's approach to these matters. The increased role of the Parliament will have implications for its relations with the Commission and the Council. The Parliament will have a stronger presence in the system and will have considerably more leverage over the Commission. Member states will be even less able to predict and control legislative outcomes because the policy process will involve bargaining and coalition-building both within the Council and with the other institutions. All of the institutional questions debated at Maastricht will be revisited in the 1990s.

The Union will have a highly fragmented system or systems of policymaking. Policymaking on foreign policy and judicial cooperation is, as has been argued above, more intergovernmental than policymaking on issues within the European Community. Although based on the Community method, policymaking on EMU is somewhat different to other EC policy areas. The roles and responsibilities of each institution differ depending on the area of activity. The Commission has a stronger executive role in some areas than others.

The Parliament's role is very varied. For example, the Parliament must give its assent to changes to the organisation of the Structural Funds but has no say in relation to 'own resources' that finance the said funds. Wrangles about the legal basis of proposed legislation are set to continue. The existence of three pillars, does not allow for a single decision-making centre to emerge which in turn means that the Union lacks political authority and its activities lack transparency. There will continue to be problems of co-ordination in foreign policy matters as the Treaty does not integrate the EC's external trade and commercial relations with the CFSP.

The Treaty of Maastricht has, if anything, increased the complexity of the Union's decision-making rules. Qualified majority voting has been extended to some aspects of environmental policy and to developing cooperation, health, consumer protection and trans-European networks. There has not been a blanket extension of qualified majority voting to all but fundamental constitutional issues. Provisions on majority voting in the EC Pillar is a follow-up to the Single Act rather than any radical departure. In very restricted circumstances and after a series of steps requiring unanimity, there is the possibility of majority voting in matters of foreign policy and judicial cooperation. The system of voting requires not just the threshold vote (fifty four votes) but these have to be cast by at least eight states. In other words, this involves a reinforced majority. Moreover,the provisions on the CFSP suggest the member states should abstain where this would assist agreement.

4. HOW DEMOCRATIC IS THE UNION?

Brigid Laffan and
Edward Moxon-Browne

There are two aspects of this question that need to be addressed. First, has the 'democratic deficit' been mitigated by the changes made at Maastricht? Second, does the introduction of Union citizenship bring Europe closer to the people?

Although the European Parliament (EP) is a key player in determining the accountability of the Union's institutions, it is the relationship between them collectively that determines whether the system, as a whole, has become democratic. The European Parliament has clearly won new powers at Maastricht but these advances are to some extent offset by new areas where the Council can take decisions on the basis of majority vote.

Although the list of matters covered by the new co-decision procedure looks fairly impressive, the Council retains the balance of power in at least two respects. First, some important areas are excluded from the co-decision process and are dealt with by a qualified majority in the Council: transport; social policy; agriculture; environmental protection; individual research programmes; and the regional and social funds. Second, the co-decision procedure contains a paragraph that allows the Council to adopt its text even where it fails to reach agreement with the parliament in conciliation. Unless the Parliament rejects the text by absolute majority within six weeks, the text becomes law. This loads the co-decision procedure in the Council's favour, because it would have to exercise a negative vote. Put simply, it has gained the right to block decisions.

The Parliament's role in the appointment of the Commission and the fact that from 1995 the term of the Commission will coincide with the Parliament's, may in the long term have a major influence on the institutional balance because it strengthens the links between the Parliament and the Commission. The Commission will become more responsive to the Parliament's interests and wishes. It will begin to have the appearance of executive responsibility to a Parliament. The ideological majority in the EP does not, as yet, affect the composition of the Commission.

The existence of three pillars and the dominance of intergovernmentalism in the pillars of foreign policy and judicial cooperation weakens the Parliament's role in these matters. The Parliament has been given at best a marginal role on foreign policy matters and an almost non-existent role in relation to judicial cooperation. Notwithstanding these lacunae, the position of the Parliament in the institutional balance has been strengthened by Maastricht.

While national governments may have emerged from Maastricht in a relatively strong position, national parliaments can draw little comfort from what was agreed. Beyond a general exhortation that exchanges of information and contacts between the European Parliament and the national parliaments should be "stepped up", and that Governments should ensure that national parliaments receive Commission proposals "in good time", there is little concrete attempt to rectify the 'democratic deficit' by involving national parliaments more closely in the work of either the European Parliament or the Union institutions. No formal or permanent body is established either alongside or within the European Parliament to guarantee that national parliamentary representatives can express views directly within the Union's decision-making system.

It is this gap in the Treaty that should be of most concern to Ireland. The position of the Oireachtas in relation to the Union's decision-making process has not improved. Although democratic accountability has arguably been strengthened at the European level, there has been no improvement at the national or local level. The Dáil has no greater control over Ministers in Brussels as a result of Maastricht; and there is no requirement that Ministers should give briefings beforehand, or report afterwards, to a European Affairs Committee on policies negotiated in Brussels.

The Committee of the Regions may have the potential to become an additional arena for democratic representation. The Committee has a purely advisory function but must be consulted on topics such as education, training, and youth; economic and social cohesion; the rules of the Structural Funds (but not their financing); trans-European networks; public health and cultural matters. This Committee can be seen as a response to the increasing assertiveness of regional identities within the Community, embracing not only those based on administrative structures such as the German Lander but also resurgent cultural militancy as in Belgium. Whether the Committee is simply an institution that can be safely ignored by national governments or can exert some influence will depend on the quality of the individuals appointed to it. Its powers are, however, negligible although, like many Community institutions in the past, it is possible that its mere existence will lead in time to it winning more responsibilities. However, this is not likely to happen overnight since national governments, jealous of their own role as 'gatekeepers' between the national and Community arenas, will act as a powerful constraint on the Committee gaining too much real influence.

In Ireland's case, the role of the Committee would be greatly enhanced if clearly defined 'regions' (with some autonomy in the determination of economic policy) were created. The country's nine representatives would then have direct links to distinct geographical areas and could articulate more authoritatively the existence of regional imbalances within the state. The principle of subsidiarity, based on the assumption that decisions are taken at the lowest effective level, could then operate in the area of regional policy.

Citizenship Of The Union

Citizenship of the Union is defined for the first time (in a Community Treaty) as "every person holding the nationality of a Member State". Thus the concept of EC citizenship is now recognised formally. Its impact is limited by the fact that member states determine their own rules regarding nationality and, therefore, who shall, and who shall not, benefit from being a 'citizen of the Union'.

Three basic rights stem from possession of Union citizenship: the right of residence in any EC country; the right to move freely within the EC; and the right of political participation in the country of residence. Some progress has been made here, even though the Maastricht proposals fall short of the ideal in at least three respects. First, although freedom of movement and residence are guaranteed, they are subject to 'measures adopted' to give effect to the Treaty. Second, as long as social security provisions and personal tax regimes continue to vary significantly between member states the theoretical freedom to live in any part of the

Union will be circumscribed by the realities of doing so. Third, as long as Union citizens are denied the right to vote in national elections in the country where they choose to live, they will, in a political sense, be second class citizens.

The right to vote in municipal and European Parliament elections is granted on the basis that EC citizens resident in a member state other than their own shall be eligible on the basis of mutual recognition of national criteria. Two limitations can be mentioned here. One is that national elections are still excluded and, arguably, it is these that matter most, if immigrants are to be incorporated into their host country's political system and participate in decisions directly affecting their daily lives. That would be a 'giant step' for the evolution of Union citizenship. The other limitation is that even rights regarding municipal and European Parliament elections are subject to the possibility that derogations (or opt-outs) may be allowed "where warranted by problems specific to a member state". This means that even the European Parliament, where uniformity could have been expected, will continue to be elected on the basis of several different electoral systems and an equally fragmented franchise.

The external 'personality' of the Union is given further recognition by the provision of consular/diplomatic protection for EC citizens in third countries where their own government has no diplomatic or consular representation. The rules for this have to be worked out among the member states by 31 December 1993, but the proposal breaks new ground and will be of immense practical value to Irish citizens working or travelling in the many third countries where no direct Irish diplomatic representation exists. However, the proposal stops short of suggesting that EC diplomatic missions, as such, should be established, although they would clearly make economic sense, and would both reflect and encourage the development of common EC policies toward third countries.

The right of EC citizens to address a petition to the European Parliament is formalised in Article 8d. More importantly, perhaps, the European Parliament is now entitled to appoint an Ombudsman to receive complaints from any citizen in the Union concerning "instances of maladministration in the activities of the Community institutions or bodies". However, the ombudsman has no power to compel an institution to change its practices, or to make compensation to an aggrieved individual. The latter has only the satisfaction of knowing that the Ombudsman will report the outcome of his findings to the European Parliament and the institution concerned.

In the absence of a fully-fledged concept of Union citizenship, the cumulative rulings of the European Court of Justice will remain one of the best safeguards of individual rights within the Union, and one of the best guarantors of the Union's 'democratic' nature. If access to legal redress is one of the essential characteristics of a democratic political system, the Union's legal framework constitutes one of the most authentic hallmarks of its legitimacy. It is therefore appropriate that the Maastricht Treaty seeks to enhance the position of Community law by exhorting national governments to enforce it with the same seriousness as they do their own domestic legislation. At the same time, the Union is required to respect fundamental rights as guaranteed by the European Convention on Human Rights (1950) to which all the Union's member states are signatories. The incorporation of this reference to the European Court of Human Rights (ECHR) will strengthen the practice, already established, whereby the Community's Court of Justice, in its own judgements, takes into account rights protected by the ECHR.

Table IV

Powers of the European Parliament

Co-Decision. Article 189b:

Single market
Consumer protection
Free circulation of workers
Right of establishment
Treatment of foreign nationals
Education
Vocational training
Research and development framework programme
Environment action programmes
Guidelines for trans-European networks
Public health
Culture

Cooperation Article 189c extended to:

Transport
European social fund implementation
Vocational training links with third countries
Standardisation of trans-European networks
Multiannual programmes in development cooperation

Assent procedure extended to:

Citizenship of the Union
Structural Funds
Cohesion Fund
Uniform electoral procedure
International agreements

THE COMMUNITY PILLAR

5. NEW POLICIES

Tony Brown

At each stage of the evolution of the European Community, the range and depth of its common policies has increased. From the limited provisions of the Coal and Steel Community in 1950 to the wide-reaching contents of the Treaty of Maastricht in 1991, there has developed a broad arena of intergovernmental policymaking in which sovereignty is pooled by the twelve member states in pursuit of the overall Community interest.

Over time, the Community's policy competence has been extended until today where there is a discernible 'European' dimension in almost every major area of public policy. At Maastricht, further significant decisions were made concerning the competence and influence of the Community in key areas of social and economic life. This chapter details these decisions and considers the potential impact of some of them.

Continuity And Change

The Treaty of Maastricht builds upon the existing body of policy provisions contained in the founding Treaties, and in particular the Treaty of Rome, and the Single European Act. Key policy areas, such as those relating to the achievement of the Single Market and to the Common Agricultural Policy, are unchanged by the decision made in Maastricht and the existing provisions stand.

At Maastricht, in fact, the outcome combined an expansion of policy competence in some areas covered by the earlier Treaties and an extension of competence into new directions in response to the rapidly changing economic, political and social environment of the 1990s. In respect of the European Community itself, the Treaty's innovative aspects are those related to:

– Citizenship of the Union

– Subsidiarity

– Economic and Monetary Union

– Economic and Social Cohesion

– Institutional Development

– New Policies.

Because of their particular importance, both for this country and for the union itself as it develops, a number of these issues are dealt with in other chapters. However, the question of New Policies is of significance since the Treaty extends the competences of the Union and of the Community in areas of great contemporary relevance.

Tasks And Competences Of The Community

Article Two of the Treaty defines the tasks of the Community as the promotion of balanced and sustainable economic growth; convergence of economic performance; protection of the environment; a high level of employment and social protection; rising standards of living and of quality of life; and economic and social cohesion.

For the purposes of carrying out those tasks, Article 3 of the Treaty sets out a list of the Activities or Competences of the Community.

Twenty headings are listed, which may be sub-divided as follows (New Policy areas are marked*):

THE ECONOMY

– Elimination of Trade Barriers

– Common Commercial Policy

– A Single Market/Free Movement of Persons, Goods, Services and Capital

– Rules Concerning Entry and Movement of Persons in the EC

– Common Agriculture Policy

- Common Transport Policy
- Competition Policy
- *Promotion of Industrial Competitiveness
- Research and Technological Development Policy
- *Establishment of Trans-European Networks.

SOCIETY AND THE CITIZEN

- Economic and Social Cohesion
- Social Policy and European Social Fund
- *Education, Training and *Culture
- *Public Health Policy
- *Consumer Protection Policy
- *Measures in the spheres of Civil Protection, Tourism and Energy
- Approximation of Laws of the Member States.

COMMUNITY AND THE WORLD

- Environment Policy
- *Development Cooperation
- Association of Overseas Countries and Territories.

Thus eight new Titles are added to the Treaty signifying that the Community now has a clear legal base on which to develop policy initiatives and to make use of Community funds to promote and implement agreed programmes and actions.

The New Policy Areas

Thus, the Community can now take steps to contribute to the establishment and development of Trans-European Networks in the essential areas of transport, telecommunications and energy infrastructures. Integration of these networks is seen as vital for the working of the Single Market. Such developments as the proposed gas and electricity grid connections between Ireland and Great Britain will benefit from this new policy area. The proposed Cohesion Fund, benefiting the four poorest member states will be a source of additional funding for activity related to the transportation element of the networks, a matter of great importance for regions which are geographically remote or peripheral within the Community.

Industrial Policy is seen as an essential element in balancing the strong emphasis on monetary provisions and criteria elsewhere in the Treaty. Stressing industrial adaptation and cooperation, initiative and enterprise and effective exploitation of technology, this policy will seek to ensure that the Community competes successfully with its world trading partners. However, the concerns of Germany which has long resisted a Community competence in this sphere are clearly reflected in a commitment to avoid any measure which might distort competition. Particular stress is laid on the promotion of the interests of small and medium-sized enterprises whose contribution to job creation is recognised as important.

In the area of Culture, the Community will encourage cooperation between the member states in matters related to heritage, history, artistic and audiovisual creativity and cultural exchanges. The inclusion of this Title in the Treaty text was claimed as a particular success by the Irish delegation at Maastricht. It is underlined that full respect for national and regional diversity in language and cultural tradition must be a central consideration in any actions of the Community.

Consumer Protection Policy is a new competence made necessary by the imminence of the Single Market. Actions will be possible in respect of protecting health, safety and economic interests of consumers and providing them with adequate information. Taking into account the existing situation in some member states, the Treaty provides that any member state may introduce or maintain protective measures which are more stringent than those proposed as common rules.

While the Community, through the Lome Conventions, has an active policy for trade with, and aid to, certain associated Third World countries, the Treaty provides a new basis for a wider policy of Development Cooperation. The objectives of this policy will give emphasis to sustainable economic and social development, integration of the developing countries into the world economy and a campaign against poverty in developing countries. Policy in this respect must, according to the Treaty text, contribute to a range of basic political goals – promoting and underpinning democracy, consolidating the rule of law and fully respecting human rights and fundamental freedoms.

A particular significant provision in this Title is the statement that "the Community shall take account of the objectives referred to . . . in the policies that it implements which are likely to affect developing countries".

The provision for measures to be taken in areas such as Tourism and Energy allow the Community institutions to develop policies on a firmer legal base. The implications of the new competences in Education and Public Health are dealt with in Chapter 8.

Expanded Policy Competences

Among policy areas in which the existing Treaty provisions have been expanded at Maastricht, is that of the Environment which has become so immensely important in the light of increased awareness of pollution, global warming and ozone depletion. It is now provided that Community policy should be directed to preserving, protecting and improving the quality of the environment and to ensuring prudent use of scarce natural resources. Particular attention is to be given to the promotion of cooperative measures at international level to deal with regional or worldwide ecological problems. Policy is to be based on the precautionary principle and on the principles that preventive action should be taken, that environmental damage should as a priority be rectified at source and that the polluter should pay. Environmental protection must be integrated into the definition and implementation of all Community policies.

Another area of extended competence is that of Research and Technological Development where the priority is now given to strengthening the technological bases of industry within the Community and to achieving effective competitiveness at the level of the world economy.

Decision-Making And Funding

Arising from this extension of competences, the Treaty provides in various Articles for improved decision-making procedures in a number of policy areas. Qualified majority voting is extended to some aspects of Environment Policy and to a number of the new Titles – Development Cooperation, Health, Consumer Protection and Trans-European Networks. The European Parliament is given so-called co-decision powers – involving an ultimate veto – under the terms of the extremely complex Article 189b, in areas such as Consumer Protection, Education, Vocational Training, Trans-European Networks, Health and Culture. Co-decision does not apply to areas such as Transport, Agriculture, Environment, Structural Funds and Research Programmes.

The effect of these provisions is to expand significantly the Community's range of policies and to move forward in terms of more efficient decision-making, through greater use of majority voting in Council. However, unanimity is retained in many areas.

The Treaty lays down that "the Union shall provide itself with the means necessary to attain its objectives and carry through its policies". The fact that each of the new competences will involve some element of financial outlay underlines the degree to which their successful implementation is dependent on the outcome of negotiations on the Delors II package.

Equally, the Community's policy development depends on the capacity of its Institutions to cope with an increased agenda and with greater legislative and administrative complexity. It is essential to avoid the potential for stagnation inherent in an overloaded policy-making system.

Further New Provisions

In addition, the Treaty contains further interesting provisions:

National Parliaments More effective contact is to be established between the European Parliament and national parliaments by means of the exchange of information and granting appropriate reciprocal facilities. National Parliaments are assured that Commission proposals will be available in good time.

Access to Information The Commission is to submit a report by the end of 1993 on the measures required to improve public access to the information available to the Community institutions. Transparency is seen to strengthen the institutions and the public's confidence in them.

European Parties   The Treaty states that "political parties at European level are important as a factor for integration . . ." The evolving political confederations represented in the European Parliament foresee an ever more important role.

Implementation of EC Law   The Court of Justice will be able to fine a member state for its failure to respect a judgement. The Commission will provide the Court with a reasoned opinion indicating the level of fine to be imposed.

In these ways the Treaty extends Community competence to bring about coherence and cooperation in policy areas of concern while respecting the principle of subsidiarity and the diversity of political culture which is the EC's great strength.

6. ECONOMIC AND MONETARY UNION

Rory O'Donnell

In agreeing a Treaty on Economic and Monetary Union (EMU) the twelve member states certainly moved the economic integration of Europe to a deeper level than ever before. However, it should be appreciated that EMU has been explicitly or implicitly on the Community's agenda for a long time. The Treaty of Rome (1957) made little reference to monetary integration but it is probable the founders of the Community expected, and intended, it would eventually become a full economic and monetary union. Indeed, the 1969 summit of Community leaders decided to create EMU by 1980. However, for a variety of reasons that effort was doomed to failure and was effectively shelved at the Paris summit of 1974.

Given this history, the current interest in EMU must be understood as, in part, a return to, or revival of, a long-standing element of the project of European union. But, why EMU now? The reasons become clear if we note, in general terms, what EMU means for the Community. First, EMU is an important step in the completion of the Single Market. Second, the move to EMU is an attempt to secure a macroeconomic environment of low inflation and steady growth. Third, it represents a significant step towards political union.

These observations go some way to explaining the current interest in EMU. Until recently the Single Market was fragmented by barriers far more significant than foreign exchange transactions and uncertainty. But the more the Single Market programme proceeded, the more people came to believe that many of its benefits would be lost if separate currencies continued to exist. For some years now low inflation and steady growth have been associated more with fixed exchange rates regimes. such as the European Monetary System, than with generalised floating.

41

Finally, while political union has been a constant theme in the Community, recent events have increased and sharpened the focus on the monetary aspects of any such union.

EMU In The New Treaty

The Treaty articles which deal with EMU may be classified into five categories: objectives; principles; instruments; rules; and transitional provisions. It is interesting that the new Treaty does not fundamentally alter the objectives of the Community as outlined in Article 2. These remain:

– growth

– a high level of employment

– price stability

– convergence of economic performance

– economic and social cohesion.

The negotiation of an EMU treaty has, however, focused attention on several principles which are now incorporated in the Treaty. These are:

– the parallel development on economic and monetary integration

– subsidiarity

– price stability as the main objective of monetary policy

– central bank independence

– sound public finances and monetary conditions

– a sustainable balance of payments

– an open market economy with free competition.

In order to pursue the above goals in accordance with these principles the Community requires certain policies and instruments. Although the full range of Community policies are relevant to pursuit of the stated objectives, the incorporation of EMU into the Treaty has resulted in the definition of new or enhanced *policy instruments* in two particular areas:

MONETARY POLICY

– the establishment of a European Central Bank and definition of its rules.

– surveillance of national macroeconomic policy and performance, formulation of broad guidelines for the economic policy of the member states and the Community and control of "excessive" budget deficits.

The Treaty defines certain *rules* governing both membership of monetary union and behaviour within it. To join EMU, a country must achieve:

– inflation close to the three best performing member states

– public finances without excessive deficits or debt

– a currency within the EMS narrow band for at least two years

– interest rates which suggest that the convergence is durable.

Within EMU and, indeed before the final stage is reached, member states must conduct their economic policies:

– as a matter of common concern and coordinate them within the Council

– with a view to contributing to the achievement of the objectives of the Community

– in accordance with the principles outlined above

– in accordance with the broad guidelines set by the European Council and the Council of Finance Ministers

– without monetary financing of budgetary deficits

– without being bailed-out by the Community

– avoiding "excessive deficits".

The Treaty, and an attached protocol, define an excessive deficit as either a government deficit significantly above three per cent of GDP, and not declining substantially and continuously towards that level, or public debt greater than sixty per cent of GDP and not approaching that value at a satisfactory pace.

The final element of the Treaty concerns the transition to EMU. Since the Delors Report of 1988, the transition to EMU has been viewed as proceeding in three stages. Stage one has already begun – involving adherence to the EMS and gradual removal of controls on the movement of capital between Community countries. Stage two involves closer coordination of macroeconomic policies and some development of the institutions which will eventually manage monetary policy and the new currency, the ecu. In the third, and final, stage exchange rates will be locked irrevocably, Community rules on macroeconomic and budgetary policy will become binding and the new European Central Bank (ECB) will prepare the transition to a single currency.

The Treaty broadly adheres to these stages. It set January 1994 as the start of stage two. That stage will see the establishment of a European Monetary Institute (EMI) rather than a European System of Central Banks (ESCB) as proposed by the Delors Report. A most important element of the Treaty is the provisions governing movement to the third and final stage. It stipulates that the European Council must decide before the end of 1996 whether a majority of member states fulfil the necessary conditions for the adoption of a single currency and, if so, set a date for the beginning of stage three. But the Treaty makes clear that "if by the end of 1997 the date for the beginning of the third stage has not been set, the third stage will start on 1 January 1999" (Article 109 J.4). At that point any number of states can proceed to EMU and those not meeting the necessary conditions will be granted a derogation. The Treaty ensures that these states cannot prevent the Community moving to the third stage and lays down that their position will be reviewed every two years.

The British Conservative Government has consistently opposed the idea of European economic and monetary union. In recognition of this the Community has designed a special procedure for the UK and attached this to the Treaty in a 'Protocol'. The procedure stipulates that the UK "shall notify the Council whether it intends to move to third stage of economic and monetary union before the Council makes its assessment" towards the end of 1996. If the UK notifies the Council that it does not intend to move to the third stage then it will be excluded from the majority and weighted majority voting procedures on matters concerning EMU. The Treaty also contains a Protocol on Denmark – in recognition of the fact that the Danish constitution may require a plebiscite prior to Danish participation in the third stage of EMU.

Interpreting The Treaty

What is the reason for these Treaty provisions? What values and interests do they serve? What compromises gave rise to them? What are the likely economic and social consequences of this type of EMU Treaty?

The last of these questions is much more difficult to answer than the rest. This is so for two reasons which should be stated explicitly at the outset. First, a Treaty merely defines the overall context within which political conflict is conducted. The actual system of EMU which emerges, (if, indeed, it does emerge) and its management for particular social and economic purposes and interests, will be determined by the political process at both national and Community level. Second, in designing and managing EMU, politicians are not, as is sometimes believed, implementing scientific principles or acting on the basis of well-established technical laws. Knowledge of the economic and social processes affected by monetary and fiscal instruments is highly imperfect and the determination of policy in the monetary area depends as much on conflicting ideologies and interests as on scientific knowledge.

In a general sense, the Treaty outlined above reflects the preoccupation with inflation, money and finance which has dominated European politics and economic policy for the last decade and a half. This is evident in the objectives, principles, instruments, rules and transition provisions. Indeed, the Treaty defines the move to a single currency rather than a full economic and monetary union, as normally understood by economists. However, within this shared preoccupation with inflation, money and finance, there are differences of emphasis and these have shaped the Treaty. Three main areas of debate can be identified: first, the aims and execution of economic policy; second, and linked to this, the institutional balance in the Community; and, third, the transition to EMU.

The Aims And Execution Of Economic Policy

Differences on the aims and execution of economic policy concern the priority given to price stability, the independence of central banks, the value of constitutional rules on deficits and debt, the degree of Community control of national policies, the roles of the central bank and 'government' in setting exchange rate policy and, generally, the degree to which policy coordination or a common economic policy is required in the Community. Overall, the Treaty proposes a system which gives a very high priority to price stability and central bank independence. It seems that to assuage German fears about losing the Deutschmark, it has been necessary to design a system which, at least in constitutional terms, gives *higher* priority to price stability and central bank independence than either the German or US systems. The desire of other governments to persuade Germany to accept EMU has shaped the Treaty and is the source of many of the anxieties which have been expressed about the plan.

A good example of this arises when we consider the Treaty rules governing national fiscal policies, both in the run-up to EMU and when the system is in place. While the German government insisted on these rules, some economists have voiced objections: that constitutional rules of this sort are arbitrary and rigid and that they are unnecessary and potentially harmful. The first anxiety has been assuaged to some degree in the Treaty. The drafting suggests, that excessive deficits will be defined within the *political* process and that in using the excessive deficit procedure, the precise figures of three per cent and sixty per cent will be guide posts rather than legally binding provisions. It would, consequently, be mistaken to believe that countries with deficits greater than three per cent or debt greater than sixty per cent will necessarily be excluded from EMU or that, once in EMU, would automatically become subject to the new "excessive deficit procedure".

However, this flexibility will not impress those who believe that such rules are unnecessary or positively harmful. They will incline to the view that with monetary policy no longer available to offset regional shocks, fiscal policy should assume a greater stabilising role.

The other side of the coin is positive coordination of member states' economic policies and the development of Community policies. Here the Treaty is much less ambitious – reflecting the great reluctance of national governments and bureaucracies to cede what they believe to be their control of policy. The result may be a somewhat unbalanced system in the sense that there may be more coherent institutions and policy on the *monetary* than on the *economic* side. This raises questions about what values, interests and social groups will be served by the single currency.

One aspect of this arises when we consider economic policy in terms of either macroeconomic policies or development of Community microeconomic policies. The central question is whether the set of Community economic policies following the Treaty will be sufficient to pursue Community goals other than price stability – especially employment, growth, competitiveness and cohesion. While the Treaty is not ambitious in this respect, no definite answer to this question can be given at this stage. It depends, to a large extent, on the manner in which policy coordination evolves in the coming years which, in turn, depends on both political and economic debate.

Another aspect concerns the balance between monetary and fiscal union. Almost all federal states and monetary unions are also fiscal unions in which there is a clear fiscal authority and tax and expenditure mechanisms which maintain inter-regional balance. The Treaty proposes monetary union without the accompanying fiscal union – yet with Community controls on national fiscal policy. The lack of fiscal union reflects the current degree of political cohesion among the governments which drafted the Treaty. It is the lack of fiscal and, therefore economic union which suggests that the language of the Treaty – 'economic and monetary union' – is somewhat exaggerated.

Institutional Issues

Economic policy ultimately depends on the institutional balance between the member states, the Council, the Commission and the Parliament. The question is whether this balance is one which produces coherent, effective, decisions. On this issue, the new Treaty can be described as conservative in the sense that it contains little institutional innovation apart from the design of the European Central Bank. Since a major motivation for EMU is political, it is pertinent to ask whether the governments have achieved sufficient political cohesion or given enough attention to the institutions which are necessary to build and sustain an EMU.

The Transition To EMU

The transitional provisions of the Maastricht Treaty, outlined above, present some difficult problems of interpretation. Two things can be stated with certainty. First, the Treaty of Maastricht embodies the *gradualist* approach advocated in the Delors Report, i.e. preference for the idea that EMU requires prior convergences of certain economic variables rather than using monetary integration to induce governments to harmonise their economic policies. Second, while the Treaty opts for a slow transition to EMU it does establish a *definite date* for the start of stage three. This constitutes a clear rejection of the British attempt to make the transition to EMU not only long but of undefined duration.

The problems of interpretation arise because the move to the single currency is premised on *prior* convergence of inflation rates, interest rates and, to an extent, budget deficits and debt. Three questions arise. One, will the single currency happen at all? Could some financial, economic or political event occur during the long transition period which would undermine the commitment of either Germany or France, or both? Two, is there a strong probability of a two-speed EMU, in which only a small number of stronger economies proceed? Three, will the simultaneous attempt of many member states to cut spending and borrowing and reduce inflation to meet the convergence criteria, imply slow, or zero, growth through the 1990s?

The Irish Focus

From an Irish perspective the basic question is whether or not to join EMU. While this is inseparable from decisions on political union four economic considerations can be identified. First, there seems little doubt that, overall, Ireland would gain from the reduction in transaction costs and exchange rate uncertainty which a single currency would bring. Second, does EMU offer the prospect of a better macroeconomic performance – low inflation and high growth – than the alternatives of the existing EMS system or an independent floating currency? Third, what is the likely regional pattern of economic activity and income in Europe and will this be made better or worse by the move to EMU as specified in the Treaty? Fourth, does the eventual decision of the U.K. on EMU have any bearing on Ireland's decision?

Apart from the decision to join, there is the question of Ireland's *ability* to join. At present Ireland meets all the conditions of entry except that on public debt. At just over 100 per cent of GDP, Ireland's public debt is clearly well above the Treaty figure of 60 per cent. It seems likely that Ireland and a number of other countries in a similar position could join EMU so long as the debt was on a steady downward course between now and the start of stage three. However, some of the questions discussed above have particular relevance in the Irish case: will small, less prosperous, countries be so anxious to prove their suitability for the single currency that they will lose any voice in the overall management of the system and, in particular, find it impossible to object to a deflationary regime?

The remaining questions concern the probable economic performance of the European Union. Irish concerns are likely to focus on growth, regional development and the European fiscal system. As a very small and open economy, Ireland can do nothing to influence the overall growth of the European economy and yet it depends on this growth to an exceptional extent. If the operation of market forces tends to create regional divergence, what policies at national and Community level will counterbalance this tendency? Given the pressure on the domestic tax system, arising from the mobility of labour and capital and the rules of EMU, will the Community develop its fiscal system in the manner found in existing federations and economic and monetary unions?

The next chapter addresses these questions by assessing the new proposals on Cohesion, set out in the Treaty and the subsequent Delors II package.

7. COHESION

Rory O'Donnell

In the language of the Community the term 'economic and social cohesion' refers to the amount of social and regional inequality between countries, regions and social groups. Since its foundation the Community had the objective of 'harmonious development'. In the 1987 Single Act this was reinforced by introduction of the concept of 'economic and social cohesion' and particular reference was made to the aim of 'reducing disparities between various regions and the backwardness of the least-favoured regions'.

The Treaty of Maastricht contains significant additional references to cohesion. Irish discussion of the new Treaty is bound to focus, to a considerable extent, on the cohesion provisions, and in order to interpret and assess them it is necessary to place them in perspective. First, it is necessary to interpret them in the light of the existing place of the cohesion issue in the Community system. Second, it is possible to see the new cohesion provisions in the context of the overall Treaty leading to deeper economic, monetary and political union. Third, it is helpful to see Community cohesion policies as only one of many factors which shape the regional pattern of economic activity and income in Europe. Consequently, this section begins with a brief account of the place of cohesion in the Community to date. The cohesion provisions in the Treaty of Maastricht are then summarised and interpreted.

Overview Of The Cohesion Issue: From The Treaty To Policies

The Treaty of Rome made no provision for a Community regional policy but it is not true that regional problems were entirely ignored at the foundation and design of the Community. It contained derogations allowing member states to grant aid to industry for the purpose of regional or sectoral development or in the face of severe crises of regional unemployment. Subsequently, several factors served to promote the development of a more genuine Community regional and social policy. The Community now has three sets of structural policies, each supported by a structural fund: the Social Fund, the Regional Fund and the structural element of the Agricultural Fund.

A significant reform of structural policy followed the Single European Act (1987). Largely at the instigation of the Irish government, the Act strengthened the Community's objective (previously in the Preamble to the Treaty of Rome) of reducing disparities between regions. This resulted in a doubling of the Structural Funds. But, nevertheless, they remained small relative to: the total Community Budget; total Community GDP; and, most significantly, to the scale of inequalities and structural problems in the European economy. The Structural Funds account for less than one quarter of the EC budget – an amount equal to only one quarter of one per cent of Community GDP.

Although there has been considerable development of both regional and social policy since the formation of the Community, the original Treaty formulation has shaped these policies, and the overall place of the cohesion question, in three important senses. First, Community social and, especially, regional policy were, and largely remain, national policies part-funded by the Community. Second, member states remained free to pursue regional and social policies which may cut across a Community cohesion objective. Third, although the objective of cohesion was, to some extent, a stated Community objective, its pursuit through national instruments meant that it was not taken into account in the main body of Community policies.

Cohesion In The Treaty Of Maastricht

The Treaty of Maastricht contains a number of new references to economic and social cohesion. These are summarised here in the order in which they appear in the Treaty.

The objective of economic and social cohesion is, for the first time, explicitly mentioned in the Preamble, or 'Common Provisions', and in Articles 2 and 3 which define the tasks and activities of the Community. Article 130b of the Single Act said that the objective of cohesion would be taken into account in the *implementation* of common policies and the

51

Single Market. In the Treaty of Maastricht this is extended to embrace the *formulation* as well as the implementation of common policies and actions (Article 130b).

A significant addition to Article 130b is the stipulation that the commission shall submit a report every three years on progress made towards economic and social cohesion. This report is to include comment on how Community measures have contributed to cohesion and shall, if necessary, be accompanied by appropriate proposals.

Some of the most significant statements appear in a *Protocol on Economic and Social Cohesion* attached to the Treaty. While this declares that the Commission and the member states are willing "to study all necessary measures" it states "that the Structural Funds should continue to play a considerable part in the achievement of Community objectives in the field of cohesion". It also reaffirms "the need for a thorough evaluation of the operation and effectiveness of the Structural Funds in 1992, and the need to review, on that occasion, the appropriate size of these funds". It is also intended to modify the operation of the Structural Funds, in two ways. One, a wider range of projects may be deemed eligible for structural fund support. Two, the Community will consider paying a higher proportion of the cost of projects where the provision of matching funds would drive member states to excessive budgetary expenditure.

The Treaty also stipulates that the Council will, before the end of 1993, "set up a Cohesion Fund providing financial contribution to projects in the fields of environment and trans-European networks in the area of transport infrastructure" (Article 130d). This fund will be available to member states which have an average income per head less than ninety per cent of the Community average.

An interesting development on cohesion is the intention, stated in the Protocol, to modify the Community's system of 'own resources' or taxation. The current system, in which a significant proportion of the Community budget is generated by VAT in each of the member states, is regressive in that poorer member states (and, indeed, individuals) can pay proportionately more than richer ones. The Protocol declares the intention to examine the system with a view to correcting the regressive elements.

A final element of the Treaty which has a bearing on Community policies for cohesion is the establishment of a new Committee of the

Regions. The committee, which will have nine members from Ireland, is to have an advisory status, somewhat similar to that of the existing Economic and Social Committee and has been described in Chapters 3 and 4.

Interpreting The Cohesion Provisions

In interpreting the cohesion provisions of the Treaty, a number of, somewhat different, perspectives need to be adopted. It is clearly necessary to consider the new provisions in the light of existing Community policies for cohesion. But it is also possible to view them with reference to the scale of regional and social inequality in the Community. Finally, it is useful to look at the cohesion provisions as part of the Community's design of a more advanced economic, monetary and political union.

While the Treaty provides for further development of Community cohesion policies it does not, in itself, mark a radical departure from the traditional approach. This is hardly surprising, since cohesion policy is primarily a matter for the political process in the Community rather than one which is dealt with in binding Treaty provisions. Consequently, the most significant factors may be the review of the Structural Funds in 1992, the negotiation of a new financial perspective for the years 1993 to 1997 and the Treaty provision for a tri-annual review of progress towards cohesion.

While the review of the Structural Funds is not complete, the Treaty itself suggests that we can expect widening of eligibility and a modulation of the rate of Community support – both responses to difficulties experienced by member states in using their existing allocations. The Commission has already set out its proposed financial perspective for 1993-97, in what has become known as the Delors II package. This suggests an increase in the Community budget from 1.2 to 1.37 per cent of Community GDP, a two thirds increase in the Structural Funds available to the least prosperous regions which, with the new Cohesion Fund, would imply a doubling of structural support to the four poorest countries (Greece, Spain, Portugal and Ireland) as a whole. This overall package, and the detailed allocation of additional resources, remain to be negotiated through the Council and the Parliament.

In the longer term, the new tri-annual review ensures that the cohesion issue remains permanently on the Community agenda. This is significant because, although the Treaty embodies the design of an 'economic and monetary union' which will enter its final phase by 1999 at the latest, the Community does not have the budgetary mechanisms which are found in almost all existing federal states and economic and monetary unions. Since these, rather than structural policies, which normally ensure inter-regional and inter-personal balance, the Community system will require careful examination and revision in the years to come. Although the concrete cohesion provisions of the Treaty of Maastricht focus on structural measures, the tri-annual review opens the possibility that, at some stage, experience or argument will prompt the development of new approaches and/or very much more substantial cohesion policies.

The new Cohesion Fund can be interpreted as, in part, a response to Spanish demands for a new inter-state compensation fund. However, the stipulation that the fund be used for projects in the field of the environment and trans-European networks suggests that other factors are also relevant. The protection of the environment and the improvement of the trans-European transport network are primarily concerns of the Commission and some richer, central, member states, rather than of poorer, peripheral, member states and regions. Consequently, the new Cohesion Fund can be seen as assistance to the poorer member states for the cost of implementing these programmes of general Community interest.

The review of the Community's taxation, or 'own resource', system constitutes a long overdue recognition of the fact that the Community's own budgetary system was cutting across its cohesion objective. While the extent of change in the system remains to be determined in the political process which sets the Community's financial perspective and annual budgets, the opening of discussion on the relevance for cohesion of the Community's budgetary system has considerable long-term potential.

It is questionable whether the establishment of the Committee of the Regions was prompted by cohesion considerations. It is more likely that pressure arose from region authorities and groups that are anxious to limit the member states' almost exclusive access to Community institutions and resources. Nevertheless, the Committee of the Regions is likely to have particular significance in less prosperous regions and member states. This is so because it is these regions which will be eligible for Structural Funds and this eligibility provides an opportunity for consultation with the regional interests represented on the new committee.

The Regional Pattern Of Economic Activity In EMU

The cohesion provisions of the Treaty must also be seen in the context of the overall set of forces which shape the regional pattern of economic activity and income in Europe. Given their size and nature, the regional pattern of economic activity and income in Europe is determined by Community cohesion policies to a very small extent. Other Community policies, such as the Single Market, the CAP, external trade policy, technology policy, environment policy, and even enlargement policy, are likely to have much more significant regional effects. National policies also have a significant impact on how a country or region performs within the international competitive environment.

Finally, and most significantly, aside from policy altogether, the regional pattern is very largely shaped by international economic forces such as industrial growth and decay, foreign direct investment, technical and organisational change and labour migration. Only when these other influences are taken into account can Community policies for cohesion, and the changes which will follow from the Treaty of Maastricht, be seen in perspective.

8. SOCIAL POLICY

Séamus Ó Cinnéide

Social Policy became known in Maastricht as the issue on which the United Kingdom parted company with the other eleven member states. In EC terminology "social policy" has had a more restricted meaning than is usually the case: it means policy in respect of workers, including workers' welfare and working conditions and workers' rights *vis-a-vis* their employers. The UK baulked at the provisions of the Draft Treaty relating to social policy and at the prospect of further EC legislation for the expansion of workers' rights, and the improvement of their welfare, throughout the Community. According to the UK, the price their employers would have to pay for EC "interference", would damage their competitive position. In the end the member states found a new and unique solution to the split, a split which reflected the earlier refusal of the UK to sign the Social Charter at the Strasbourg Council in 1989.

A total impasse between the UK and the other member states on the inclusion in the Treaty of the section on social policy, which greatly expanded the Social Charter, was averted by a decision of the Eleven to conclude an agreement among themselves without the UK. A protocol was agreed by all member states which noted the decision of the Eleven and permitted them to make use of the institutional structures of the Community to implement the agreement which consists of the articles on social policy proposed in the original Draft Treaty.

The Agreement
The Agreement on Social Policy makes a number of significant changes. Firstly, the constitutional basis of EC action in relation to social policy is to be expanded: social policy comes to have a wider, more familiar,

meaning. Going beyond the provisions of the existing Treaties, the Agreement sets out the objectives of Community social policy as "the promotion of employment, improved living and working conditions, proper social protection, dialogue between management and labour, the development of human resources with a view to lasting high employment and the combating of exclusion". This means the Community will have the power to address a wider range of pressing social concerns of all the member states.

Secondly, while some decisions on social policy (e.g. in relation to social security, procedures for the representation of workers and employers and conditions of employment for third-country nationals) can only be taken by the member states acting unanimously, other decisions (e.g. in relation to working conditions, equality between men and women, consultation of workers and programmes dealing with exclusion or poverty) can be taken by qualified majority voting. This may lead to long overdue progress, for example, in relation to worker participation, since in the past, some progressive initiatives were blocked by the threatened veto of one or two countries.

Thirdly, in relation to those issues covered by the Agreement the two sides of industry, employers and trades unions, will have an enhanced role. The "social partners" will have to be consulted on all initiatives in the social policy field. Furthermore, the social partners at EC level – UNICE, ETUC and CEEP – may take the initiative themselves, and any agreement made between them can be ratified by the Community, in effect turning it into EC law, or implemented by the social partners at the national level. This had been agreed by the social partners themselves just before Mastricht and the Treaty in effect incorporated their agreement.

Significance

The significance of the Agreement for workers may be gauged from the terms of a statement issued by the Executive Committee of the ETUC and calling on the trade union movement to support the ratification of the Treaty:

> The Agreement among the Eleven . . . contains the minimum demands which the ETUC considered acceptable, notably as regards the extension of Community powers (particularly on working

conditions, information and consultation and the fight against exclusion), as well as the qualified majority voting procedures to adopt measures relating to these aspects.

The Agreement on Social Policy will apply to Ireland as one of the eleven signatories to the Agreement. Some may argue that in due course this may place intolerable burdens on Irish employers and that our neighbour, not similarly burdened, will have a competitive advantage. But given our commitment to economic and social cohesion we could hardly opt out of general improvements in workers' conditions; and in any case it is doubtful if further EC legislation, which will have to take account "of the diverse forms of national practices... and the need to maintain the competitiveness of the Community economy" will materially affect productivity or investment decisions in the UK. For instance, it is unlikely that multinational companies from outside the EC would decide to locate in the UK simply because of lower labour costs which may or may not continue into the future; and agreements made by joint industrial councils of multinational companies operating throughout the EC will hardly exclude the British workers of those companies.

Interpretation

But the Maastricht decisions must be considered against the background of EC policy generally. Until now the European Community has been seen almost exclusively as an economic union, and it has been criticised, rightly, for its lack of an overall social policy. The purpose of the Community has been defined in terms of economic development, and comparatively little attention has been given to *social* development: the equitable sharing of the fruits of economic development and the attainment of broader objectives which have to do with personal welfare, local development and social solidarity.

And yet social objectives have been there from the beginning: equal pay for men and women; retraining for workers made redundant; and transferability of welfare entitlements for migrant workers. Disparate programmes and initiatives, with varied origins in EC law, were consolidated and boosted in the EC Social Charter adopted by eleven member states in 1989 (as mentioned above, the exception was the UK). Commitments were made in this document and are being followed through by the EC Commission in an Action Programme, consisting of a wide range of policy proposals, which predates Maastricht and will continue to involve all twelve member states. In other words, there will be two overlapping sets of policy issues and decisionmaking procedures: those already covered in previous Treaties and in train before Maastricht and those covered in the new Agreement on Social Policy. As the ETUC points out: "Problems will obviously arise because of the complexity of a situation where two texts exist on the same subjects. This might happen, for instance, with health and safety measures arising from two different legal sources, and for equal opportunities which might be interpreted repressively and hence, at the end of the day, reinforce discrimination".

There are still further areas of uncertainty. The Agreement mentions Community competence relating to "working conditions"; but what does that include and exclude? There may be scope for some creative drafting in influencing which precise issues fall within the Agreement, and, of them, which have to be decided unanimously and which can be decided by a qualified majority. The majority voting system would suit Ireland in some cases and not in others. And how will the social partners at the EC level interpret their remit, and how much initiative will they take? All this remains to be seen. On this last issue, a representative of Irish employers is optimistic that "operated properly, a resurgent social dialogue would mean the achievement of worthwhile economic and social programmes on a basis other than through the use of broadly-based, burdened-with-detail directives in the old style".

It is difficult to generalise even about social policy issues covered by the Agreement. There are widely contrasting positions in relation to different policy areas. For instance, from the beginning the EC's commitment to equal pay has had a very far-reaching influence on women's rights by requiring the reform of national legislation relating to equality between men and women. Given that EC initiatives in this area are to be decided in the future by a qualified majority further progress can be made. The field of social security is very different. There have been agreements to ensure that people do not lose out on entitlements by moving from one country to another, and proposals for convergence, or voluntary harmonisation, in social security between member states. Social security issues will, however, continue to be decided on unanimously and the harmonisation or standardisation of social security is not at all on the agenda for the present.

Extension Of Social Policy
In the past there has also been a whole range of smaller EC programmes

and activities for disadvantaged groups such as the poor, the handicapped and migrants. In the Agreement the fact that "the combating of social exclusion" was written into the objectives of the Community means that social exclusion, and, in particular, exclusion from the labour force, can now be the focus of EC policies: the EC will be able to deal with poverty issues much more than in the past. Thus a policy area which was first brought to the Community's negotiating table by the Irish government in the early 1970s, with the first EC Poverty Programme, has now been given Treaty status. A major Commission conference on policies and programmes to combat social exclusion has already (April 1992), highlighted the importance of this development.

In addition to areas covered by the Agreement on Social Policy, Maastricht also represents an extension of the definition of social policy generally, and of EC competence in other areas. For instance, there is the European Social Fund (ESF) which was designed to achieve some redistribution between member states by financing training and retraining for young people coming on the labour market, and for those who are unemployed. The operation of all the Structural Funds will be reviewed during 1992 with a view to ensuring that they become more effective in achieving economic and social cohesion. Another protocol to the Treaty, the Protocol on Economic and Social Cohesion, may have a more profound effect on how the Social Fund operates. This protocol declares an intention "to allow a greater margin of flexibility in allocating financing . . . to specific needs not (now) covered". This opens up the possibility of ESF funding for wider social service programmes in certain member states.

Secondly, the EC has developed over the years certain limited functions in relation to education and public health, but these had a narrow legal basis. In the new Treaty there is a whole new section on education which puts it more clearly on the EC agenda (Article 126). The formal emphasis is on promoting the European dimension in education at the national level, and on facilitating cross-national exchanges among teaching staffs and students, activities which are already well established.

But the terms "supporting and supplementing" the action of member states in relation to education could open up wider possibilities. Already in Ireland NESC has suggested that education generally should be grant-aided from Brussels, since we are feeding into a European labour market.

While this will still not be possible, because EC competence will continue to relate mainly to training, widely defined, a future expansion of competence could be envisaged.

There are also new provisions on health policy in the Treaty (Article 129). Heretofore, the EC remit in relation to health matters has been limited: there have been EC education campaigns in relation to cancer and AIDS, and there has been cooperation between member states on research. Now, as in the case of education, the Community accepts a certain responsibility in the health field within its constitution. Again this opens up the possibility of a wider EC health services policy in the future.

There is no doubt but that EC competence in the wider social policy field, and not just in relation to workers as workers, is expanding. The process is a gradual one, and builds on existing programmes and activities. It is probably an irreversible process, not least because of the co-decision provisions which will apply in many social policy areas, and which give greater powers to the European Parliament.

THE INTERGOVERNMENTAL PILLARS

9. COMMON FOREIGN AND SECURITY POLICY

Patrick Keatinge

The European Community has become an increasingly important entity in world politics since the mid-1980s. The unification of Germany in 1990 – itself the catalyst for the Inter Governmental Conference on Political Union – was a reflection of a much wider transformation, centred on the collapse of the Soviet Union and its associated 'bloc'. However, although the militarised confrontation of the Cold War is over, security is still a major concern; it has not proved possible simply to collect the 'peace dividend' and treat foreign policy as a mere gloss on global economic management. The negotiations leading to the Treaty of Maastricht started against the background of the Gulf War and ended with the civil war in Yugoslavia still unresolved.

In spite of arguments that these developments provided an incentive for radical changes in the way the EC and its member states should deal with the rest of the world, the Treaty of European Union is cast in a familiar mould. Three separate elements can be identified:

– external trade is covered in the amended EEC Treaty, in its own chapter on Common Commercial Policy. This tidies up some of the details of the previous provisions, but does not involve substantial change

– development Cooperation for the first time is consolidated in a similar way, in the 'Community pillar'. It is decided by qualified majority voting and is subject to the European Parliament's cooperation procedure. However, it remains complementary to national policies, and the changes made were not regarded as controversial

– the coordination of foreign policy is, however, treated in a different way. The previous legal base, Title III of the Single European Act, has been repealed altogether and is replaced by new provisions on Common Foreign and Security Policy (CFSP).

The negotiations on this part of the Treaty were difficult, and their outcome merits especial attention since it raises two important questions. The first concerns the conduct of foreign policy. Do the member states retain their legal independence in this regard, or is there to be a Union foreign policy? Here we must look closely at the decision-making procedures. The second major issue is that of defence, which in turn leads to the question of neutrality.

Continuity And Change

The provisions on a Common Foreign and Security Policy form a separate 'pillar' of the Treaty, called 'Title V', consisting of Article J. Although there is an exhortation in the Common Provisions (Article C) to ensure the consistency of the Union's 'external activities as a whole', the legal character of this pillar is intergovernmental rather than supranational. This follows conventional international practice; it is a notable absentee from the subjects which come under the jurisdiction of the European Court of Justice (ECJ). We have here a very much looser form of 'common policy' than those found in the Community pillar, such as the Common Agricultural Policy.

The assertion of the new Union's international identity is one of its major overall objectives, referred to in both the Preamble and Article B in the Common Provisions. This is spelled out more fully in Article J.1, in a series of general objectives which refer to the values and obligations associated with the United Nations and the Conference on Security and Cooperation in Europe (CSCE). Two points are significant here. Previously such objectives were expressed in non-binding political declarations rather than in a legal text. More important, the scope of the Union is to cover *all* areas of security, whereas Title III of the Single European Act referred only to 'economic and political aspects of security'. This implicit exclusion of military issues has disappeared, but the more comprehensive scope envisaged is then weakened by two factors. First, as we shall see below, the terms of any future defence policy remain to be negotiated in a further Inter Governmental Conference. Second, the Union's objectives must be interpreted in the light of the decision-making procedures to be employed.

There is a strong element of continuity with Title III so far as the policy process is concerned.The attempt to agree on common positions by consensus – European Political Cooperation – re-emerges in more confident language as "systematic cooperation" in Article J.2. As was the case in the Single European Act, there is an exhortation not to prevent consensus emerging: member states "will, to the extent possible, avoid preventing a unanimous decision where a qualified majority exists in favour of that decision". Of course, the judge of what is possible remains, in the last resort, the individual member state. Moreover, the exhortation is not in the main body of the text, nor even in the form of a legally binding protocol. It is expressed as a Declaration of the Conference, which is not legally binding.

There is also a continued rationalisation of the institutional arrangements which have evolved over the last twenty one years. The Commission's position as the 'extra participant' is recognised more fully. The small EPC Secretariat is now absorbed into the Council Secretariat, which is responsible for the rest of the Union's business; however, the Political Committee of the foreign ministries' Political Directors retains a distinct role. The Council Presidency is still responsible for the political management of the process.

Majority Voting? – A Contested Experiment

None of these measures could account for the contentious nature of the negotiations on the CFSP. That could very largely be ascribed to the attempt to introduce majority voting into foreign policy for the first time. Where the member states have 'important interests in common' a new concept of 'joint action' has been introduced in Article J.3.This lays out an elaborate series of decisions, on the basis of general guidelines agreed (by unanimity) by the heads of government in the European Council. The foreign ministers, in the Council, then agree (again by consensus) whether an issue is to be decided under the joint action procedure. At this stage they must be quite specific in defining the scope, objectives, and means to be employed. Only in that context can they decide which decisions are to be taken by a qualified majority (of at least 54 votes in favour, cast by at least 8 member states). Such decisions are legally binding.

In principle, joint action represents a departure from the conventional position in which the individual state retains its formal independence with regard to its foreign policy. That said, this innovation would seem to be remarkably constrained in practice. It is not the normal mode of decision-making, but rather is seen as a tentative experiment. The procedure only arrives at qualified majority voting at the end of a chain of consensus decisions at the highest political levels. The Treaty is well stocked with safeguards (from the point of view of individual states) or loopholes (from the point of view of would-be federalists). There is provision for states being able to act on their own to some extent, on the ground of 'imperative need' [Article J.3 (6)]. Issues with defence implications are *excluded altogether* [Article J.4 (3)]. The President of the Commission, Jacques Delors, for his part has simply described joint action as 'unworkable', as an unnecessarily cumbersome procedure restricted to trivial matters.

Indeed, it is not very clear what issues will be treated under this joint action procedure. Both before and during the negotiations attempts were made to draw up lists of appropriate areas for joint action, and one such list was on the table at Maastricht, though it did not eventually appear among the Declarations annexed to the Treaty. It contained mostly preventive security measures, such as arms control and CSCE matters – the so-called agenda of 'soft security' – plus a commitment to come up with some more ideas by the next meeting of the European Council. The impression is given of an unresolved debate among professional diplomats who would much rather explore the possibilities of joint action on a case-by-case basis.

That might take some time. At this juncture, it is difficult to see governments, especially the larger ones, abandoning their freedom of manoeuvre on a point of substance. The British government has made no secret of its negative attitude in this regard. The French foreign minister has assured his parliament that France is not about to give up its 'great power' prerogatives, such as an independent nuclear force or its permanent seat on the UN Security Council. The former is not in any case subject to the Treaty of Maastricht. The latter illustrates the limits of the CFSP. Article J.5 requires Union member states in the Security Council to "concert" i.e. consult among themselves. Those with *permanent* seats are called on to defend the interests of the Union – but without prejudice to their special UN responsibilities. Thus, in circumstances where their vote is essential if the Security Council is to act, France and the United Kingdom retain a power of decision independent of the Union. A federal union, on the other hand, would seek a permanent seat of its own.

Meanwhile the the largest state in the new Union, Germany, remains outside the UN's 'Big Five' and persists with its repudiation of nuclear military capability. Nevertheless, it is widely recognised that one of the most important questions facing both Germany and its neighbours is how it comes to terms with its enhanced diplomatic potential. As the negotiations were being concluded in Maastricht, Germany was taking the lead on the issue of the recognition of Croatia and Slovenia, but in a way which showed some impatience with the need to maintain solidarity with its partners.

On the whole, then, it seems that the provisions on a Common Foreign and Security Policy represent a consolidation of existing practice rather than a radical innovation. In legal terms the member states are still independent; in political terms their freedom of action depends on their own political resources. This situation continues to allow scope to the larger states to treat the Union in a cavalier fashion, should they so wish. From the point of view of the small states, it is open to question whether they might not in general exert more influence on their larger partners – and thus on the Union – in a policy regime which was *more* constraining than that of Article J.

In the light of the procedural uncertainties in the CFSP – and indeed of the uncertain world the procedures must deal with – the political accountability of foreign policy assumes an even greater importance than usual. At first sight the European Parliament seems to be in much the same position as before. It is consulted and informed, but its success in exerting influence still depends largely on its ability to keep its own house in order. Two innovations may, however, give it additional leverage. Development Cooperation policy now comes under the cooperation procedure and, more importantly, operational expenditure under the CFSP provisions may be charged to the Community budget. In cases where there are significant operational costs – the deployment of EC monitors in Yugoslavia is an example of how these might arise – this could allow the European Parliament to influence foreign policy through its general budgetary powers.

However, much of the responsibility for holding the Union to account for the conduct of foreign policy still rests, indirectly, with national parliaments. They are still the institutions in which the members of the Council – national governments – can be called to account. Whether they equip themselves to perform this task is, of course, entirely up to them; repeated demands in the Dáil for a foreign affairs committee or an expanded European affairs committee suggest that there is room for improvement in this regard. The government's stated intent to establish such a committee may thus prove to be an important complement to the measures of democratic accountability contained in the Treaty of Maastricht.

Defence For The Future?

The Irish government's White Paper of April 1970, on possible EEC membership, recognised that "as the Communities evolve towards their political objectives, those participating in the new Europe thereby created must be prepared to assist, if necessary, in its defence". This political commitment has rarely been pursued with enthusiasm in a country which has adopted a stance of military neutrality, and in which military alliances are often seen as inherently militaristic rather than defensive. This is perhaps the most obvious reservation in Ireland about a federal union – for collective defence is at the heart of federal government, and has historically been a major motivation for confederations. Does the Treaty of Maastricht require a change of mind and policy in this regard?

The immediate answer is 'no' – there is no commitment to military alliance in the Treaty. However, for the first time since the French National Assembly rejected the European Defence Community in 1954, defence is explicitly included as a future objective of European Union. The Preamble, Article B of the Common Provisions, and Article J.4 all refer to "the eventual framing of a common defence policy, which might in time lead to a common defence". All of this is in the context of a commitment to convene a further Inter Governmental Conference in 1996 to raise the question formally [Final Provisions, Article N (2)]. In short, defence *is* on the medium term horizon.

The Treaty reference to 'a common defence policy' being framed in 1996 implies that the very nature of the policy has yet to be agreed. The additional reference to 'a common defence', on the other hand, concerns an actual instrument of collective defence – an alliance organisation, with its own strategic doctrine, integrated command, and force deployments. It is no accident this eventual possibility appears in such tentative language. The inclusion of both phrases in the Treaty may be confusing, but they are there to accommodate the two sides in one of the most divisive arguments during the negotiations. A 'Europeanist' group, led by France, pressed for an immediate defence role for the new Union; the 'Atlanticists', led by the United Kingdom, sought to preserve NATO as the central institution for European defence. The Treaty of Maastricht does not resolve this argument, but rather puts it off until 1996.

Neutrality Survives

This stand-off has important consequences for a state like Ireland, which is reluctant to develop the military or 'hard security' side of the Union. Indeed, Ireland's position is reinforced by the provision, in Article J.4(4), that the Union's security policy does not prejudice "the specific character of the security and defence policy of certain Member States". The phrase 'certain member states' covers any individual signatory of the Union Treaty, and could presumably accommodate other neutral states which join the Union. Although the same article goes on to say that Union policy shall "respect" the obligations of "certain Member States under the North Atlantic Treaty", and "be compatible with" its policies, the net effect of this clause is to permit all member states to carry on as before. Again, the absence of an existing defence policy for the Union is evident. Irish neutrality survives, for now.

Nevertheless, it is clear that the issue of collective defence can no longer be wished out of existence. Two broad questions will merit close attention over the next few years. The first concerns the position of the United States. During the pre-Maastricht negotiations the American administration underlined its determination to maintain NATO as the authoritative defence entity, and American military predominance was demonstrated in the Gulf War. Yet that event also suggested limits to the American role as the only superpower; the US was under considerable financial pressure and confined its action to the expulsion of Iraq from Kuwait. Subsequently, the American government applied its diplomatic leadership selectively, being very active with regard to the Middle East peace process, but remaining in the background during the Yugoslav civil war.

This may be no more than the skilful shepherding of resources, but it may be that the US, too, has been exhausted by the Cold War which helped destroy its former superpower adversary. The desire and ability of future American administrations to take the dominant role in a European military alliance cannot be taken for granted in the face of competing domestic and foreign policy demands. Probably the one question that would encourage them to stay 'in Europe' would be continuing instability in the countries of the former Eastern bloc, especially in view of the complex nuclear dangers that might develop there.

The second major question is a more fundamental one, concerning the nature of a future common defence policy: what is the Union to be defended against, and by what means? Defence policy for most

European states, including the continental neutrals, used to be defined in terms of the confrontation between the two military blocs. That situation, with its attendant perceptions of threat, has now disappeared. In its place is a number of security problems, many of which are neither military in character nor primarily inter-state in form. However, it is also clear that inter-state violence, either inside or outside the European region, cannot be ruled out.

The wide array of new challenges, in conjunction with the residue of some old ones, requires a comprehensive reappraisal of the content of defence policy. The concept of 'common security', which emphasises diplomatic and economic measures in an inclusive network of security institutions, is a more appropriate guide to future policy than the replication of traditional alliances. The policy of the European Union cannot be framed in isolation; rather it is but one element in a broader canvas, including a reformed UN, the CSCE, and other regional institutions. Nor does the former emphasis on a predominantly military response seem appropriate.

Nevertheless, the proposition that a common defence policy does not require *any* collective military commitment does not look like obtaining majority support among European governments. Those member states close to actual or potential conflict continue to seek guarantees of mutual assistance, as indeed do some former members of the defunct Warsaw Pact. So long as nuclear weapons exist, whether in Europe or elsewhere, the dilemmas posed by nuclear deterrence will remain in some form. These awkward questions look like staying on the agenda until 1996, and well beyond.

European Union And The WEU

Although the definition of defence lies in the future, the Treaty of Maastricht nevertheless envisages a possible role for the European Union in security matters with defence implications. In such circumstances the Union can call on another union, the Western European Union (WEU), to act on its behalf.

To understand what this means, it is necessary to look more closely at the WEU. Formally, it is a military alliance consisting of nine members, all of which happen to be EC member states. In practice, its military significance has always been negligible, since its operational tasks have been subsumed into NATO. Its real importance has been as an occasional political catalyst, a device which at infrequent intervals has been employed to resolve problems within the western alliance. Its foundation treaty marked the good faith of the European partners in the creation of NATO in the late 1940s, and it served as the legitimator of German incorporation into NATO in the mid-1950s. Since the mid-1980s, it has been in effect an institutional arena for testing the respective merits of the Atlanticist and Europeanist concepts of collective defence.

The WEU continues in the latter role in the Treaty of Maastricht, where it sits uneasily in both camps. In the Treaty itself, it is described rather tentatively as "an integral part of *the development* of the European Union", suggesting it is not quite there yet [Article J.4 (2): author's emphasis]. In a separate Declaration agreed by the WEU states, and annexed to the Treaty, it appears as "a means to strengthen the European pillar of the Atlantic Alliance". This goes on to stress that so far as alliance issues are concerned, it is the "Alliance which will remain the *essential forum* for consultation among its members" (author's emphasis). The Declaration's call for more cooperation on operational matters underlines the WEU's existing weakness in this respect.

So far as the new European Union is concerned, notwithstanding the very large overlap in membership, the WEU is still an autonomous organisation. The European Union 'requests' the WEU to act on its behalf, a request which is decided by consensus. Formally, therefore, a member state which, like Ireland, does not want to be involved in military action can actually prevent the Union going down that road. In practice, it is very unlikely that any one state, and especially a small state, would feel able to avail of this prerogative against all its partners, all the time. However, so long as differences persist between Atlanticists and Europeanists within the WEU, it is unlikely that Ireland would be isolated in this way.

That does not preclude the WEU being associated with the Union's policy on 'soft security' issues. This has already occurred in effect, through the WEU's coordination of aspects of the humanitarian intervention to protect the Kurds in northern Iraq in April 1991. In this case the WEU's legal capacity to act outside its members' territory allowed it to act where NATO as such could not. It is also likely that closer links will be established between the institutions of the two unions. The WEU Declaration refers to synchronising meetings and encouraging closer cooperation between the respective parliamentary assemblies, though its decision to move its Council and Secretariat to Brussels is as much a gesture to NATO as it is to the new Union. The latter's Treaty is more reticent on this aspect, simply referring to "the necessary practical arrangements" [Article J.4 (2)].

Ireland And The WEU

What does all of this mean for Ireland, and in particular for Irish neutrality? On the latter point, in the short term it means very little. Ireland is not a party to the WEU Declaration annexed to the Treaty of Maastricht, and does not take on any military obligations in the Treaty itself.

However, the continuing flux of international politics is bound to put pressure on all European states, including the neutrals, to clarify and adapt their positions on security and defence issues. The Cold War orthodoxies about alignment and non-alignment are inadequate; to see the WEU, or its parent body NATO, as fixed for ever in their Cold War mould is to neglect the extent to which they, like the EC, are already being transformed. Within two weeks of the Maastricht summit, NATO was establishing an institutional relationship with its former adversaries, in the North Atlantic Cooperation Council (NACC). The WEU's own treaty may be open to change in 1998, and the timing of the 1996 review clause in the Treaty of Maastricht was partly determined by the possibility of such a review.

The extraordinary changes of the last few years represent a window of opportunity to reshape world politics in a way which has not been possible for nearly half a century. Ideas about bringing the instruments of war under control – measures for nuclear non-proliferation, restraining arms exports, and peacekeeping – are nearer the top of the agenda. There is some evidence of a new convergence of purpose between the UN, the CSCE, and the traditional alliances, in which all these organisations may be able to operate as complementary elements in an overall system of common security. It remains to be seen whether these institutions, or the governments they represent, can respond effectively to this opportunity; likewise, the European Union's role in security policy requires further definition.

In this context what options are open to Ireland? One possibility is to preserve the stance of neutrality at all costs. The terms of the Treaty leave this open. Even in the definition of a defence policy for the Union, arising out of the agreed Inter Governmental Conference in 1996, it may be possible to argue that Ireland (or any other member state) should not be a full participant in the arrangements for collective defence. However, one consequence of such a strategy would probably be the creation of a formal two-tier system, in which Ireland would be in the second tier, with the attendant risk of seriously weakening the state's bargaining position on *all* the Union's policies.

Another negative consequence of such an approach cannot be discounted. The insistence on the letter of neutrality might have the paradoxical effect of reducing Ireland's capacity to influence the development of the European Union in the way in which supporters of neutrality would prefer. The argument that the Union should not develop into a military superpower with ambitions to project its power 'out of area' is likely to be more effectively advanced from within rather than outside the context of a collective defence policy. In order to promote effectively the values associated with neutrality, such as the minimum resort to force, the diplomatic inhibitions inherent in neutrality might have to be relinquished. In order to influence the scope and ethos of a new alliance, is it necessary to be a member?

This dilemma does not have to be resolved just yet. It is nonetheless foreshadowed in a further Declaration of the WEU states issued at Maastricht, which invites all members of the new European Union to join the WEU or take up observer status. Ireland has already adopted the latter option on an *ad hoc* basis on three occasions (19 and 30 September 1991, on the Yugoslav crisis, and at the simultaneous meeting at Maastricht). To accept this invitation as a matter of routine may appear uncongenial to those who see the WEU as the seed-bed of incipient Euro-militarism. It might, on the other hand, simply provide an opportunity to form a considered judgement as to whether such a view had any basis in fact.

Strengthening The Confederation

Taking the CFSP pillar in the round, it is clear that it does not look like the basis for a federal foreign policy. Although the principle of such a policy finds some expression in the objectives and the procedure for joint action, the new provisions are more appropriately seen as the strengthening of existing confederal arrangements. Decision-making is still intergovernmental where it matters. Defence is at most contracted out to a separate body which itself has not yet established a clear role. This arrangement even falls short of the practice of many conventional confederations.

Moreover, Article J covers only one aspect of the Union's overall character as an international actor. That is still more accurately described in terms of 'civilian power', rather than the trappings of a military superpower. The Union's influence in the world will be based on its *economic* significance, and will more often than not be exercised by the economic policy instruments which are allowed for in the Treaty's first pillar. The Common Foreign and Security Policy serves as a complement to these activities, not as an alternative to them.

Finally, it is necessary to emphasise the tentative nature of the Union's role in the world, if for no other reason than the continuing instability in world politics. A particularly important aspect of this period of change, which is likely to exert a strong influence on the way in which the Common Foreign and Security Policy evolves, is the demand for membership of the Union itself. Thus, although it was not on the table at Maastricht, the question of enlargement is examined in Chapter 11.

10. COOPERATION IN JUSTICE AND HOME AFFAIRS

Brigid Laffan

Cooperation on judicial matters and what is called in the Treaty 'Home Affairs' forms a third pillar of the Union. Police cooperation on a European and international scale is nothing new, but the goal of a barrier-free Europe raises important questions about the management of a range of sensitive issues including asylum, visas, and border crossings for the member states. A central feature of the 1992 Programme is the removal of all physical barriers or border controls from the first of January 1993 on the Community's internal borders. This implies that the Community's 320 million citizens will have the right to cross borders without routine checks.

It also implies that the member states must reach agreement on how to deal with third country nationals. Immigration is an increasingly sensitive issue in a number of member states. There is some evidence that right wing parties may be strengthening their electoral position in a number of countries (notably, France, Belgium and Germany), adopting an anti-immigration policy stance. North Africa, where population projections suggest that the working population is set to increase from 67 million in 1990 to some 106 millions by the end of the decade, and Eastern Europe are the two main sources of potential migrant workers. External pressure and the logic of the Single Market make immigration policy a core area of Community activity for the 1990s.

The member states have been cooperating in this field under the Trevi system since 1976. The group met at ministerial, senior official and working party level. A working party, Trevi 92, was established to examine the police and security aspects of 1992. This led to a 1990 convention on asylum seekers and further work on visa requirements. The continental states have anticipated much of the work on the free movement of people with agreement to the Schengen system in 1990. The Schengen Treaty allows for the free movement of people among the continental EC states apart from Denmark. It provides for a 'Schengen Information System' to allow for the exchange of information about suspects and stolen goods among the national police forces and also has provisions on 'hot pursuit'. Policy cooperation in this field may in time lead to a 'Euro-FBI' and joint police work.

The sensitivity of the issues involved for national security and the traditional secrecy of Justice ministries means that the Treaty of Maastricht does little more than codify existing practice within an intergovernmental framework. The scope of cooperation in this field is as follows:

– asylum policy

– rules governing the crossing by persons of the external borders of the member states

– immigration policy re nationals of third countries

– entry and movement of third country nationals

– residence of third country nationals

– combating unauthorised immigration

– combating drug addiction

– combating fraud

– judicial cooperation in civil matters

– judicial cooperation in criminal matters

– customs cooperation

– police cooperation – European Police Office (Europol).

The main focus of this pillar is on combating serious crime and on putting in place arrangements for dealing with third country nationals in terms of their access to the territory of the member states and their rights when in the Community.

Cooperation will be based on joint positions, joint action and conventions. The Commission does not have a sole right of initiative but must be 'fully associated with the work' in this sphere. The Parliament has a limited right to be consulted. The situation concerning majority voting is extremely complicated. In line with the provisions on a CFSP, there is provision for 'joint action'. Such measures may be implemented on the basis of a qualified majority.

Moreover, measures implementing the provisions of conventions, may be adopted by a majority of two thirds of the member states. Even the system of majority voting is somewhat different to the orthodox or EEC provisions. A qualified majority remains at fifty four votes but must be cast by a least eight states. Unanimity remains the dominant decision-making rule in this sphere. Although judicial review is not a feature of intergovernmental cooperation in the Union, conventions may give the European Court of Justice jurisdiction to interpret such conventions and to rule in disputes.

The provisions on judicial cooperation must be read in conjunction with Article 100c of the EC part of the Treaty. This covers matters relating to the granting of visas to third country nationals. Article 100c provides for an emergency response from the Community in the event of a sudden movement of people. Although unanimity remains the decision rule, it is envisaged that qualified majority will replace unanimity after the first of January 1996 and that before this date, the member states will put in place a uniform format for visas. The provisions of Article 100c may be extended to other matters outlined in the provisions on judicial cooperation provided that the member states are agreeable to this.

The Treaty's provisions in this field are largely intergovernmental. However, there are opportunities to adapt these provisions so that they resemble the Community method of decision-making. Eventually this pillar may merge with the Community pillar but such an evolution remains in the hands of the member states.

EUROPE AFTER MAASTRICHT

11. ENLARGEMENT

Tony Brown

While the Treaty contains no new reference to Enlargement, it is now clear that this will be a central political challenge for the newly-formed Union in the decade ahead. An initial phase of enlargement – involving Austria, Sweden and Finland – may be expected within three or four years to be followed by more EFTA states and, later in the decade by Hungary, Czechoslovakia and Poland. Others will surely follow.

Significantly, a week after the 'Twelve' had agreed the details of the Maastricht Treaty another important European text was signed in The Hague. Forty four countries, including those of the Commonwealth of Independent States (CIS) were among the signatories of the European Energy Charter. The separate appearance on such a stage of Kirghiztan, Turkmenistan, Moldavia and a dozen others underlined the massive changes which have taken place in Europe in no more than three years. And, in late January, ten of the CIS republics were admitted to membership of the CSCE at its Prague meeting while Croatia and Slovenia were given observer status.

Presidency Conclusions

Reflecting the reality of this change, the Presidency Conclusions of the European Council made specific and significant reference to Enlargement. It was noted that a number of applications are now on the table and decided that formal negotiations could begin "as soon as the Community has terminated its negotiations on Own Resources. . ." This implies that formal negotiations with Austria and Sweden, and probably Finland, will commence later this year, or early in 1993, when the Delors II package on the financing of the Community has been dealt with.

The European Council recognised the serious institutional issues which arise in connection with further enlargement, and the related financial and political questions. Having regard to these matters the European Council has instructed the Commission to examine in detail all aspects of Enlargement and to report to the Lisbon European Council meeting in June 1992. In particular, the instruction to the Commission laid emphasis on the "implications for the Union's future development."

The Portuguese Presidency has indicated that the preparation of a strategy to deal with Enlargement would be among its top priorities. The Lisbon European Council will receive the Commission report on Enlargement after which it should be possible to begin negotiations with the initial applicants.

Evolution Of The Community

Enlargement poses fundamental questions about the future role and character of the Union. It has been suggested that one of the tasks of the Lisbon European Council will be to define the Union's vision "of the role that it intends to play in the world and the priorities which it assigns itself to exercise it".

Differing concepts exist, on the one hand of a Europe ready to "shoulder its share of the military responsibilities of the old nations which have left their mark on history" and, on the other, of Europe as a Zone of Peace, "in a sense . . . the first of the world's civilian centres of power". Equally, it is possible to identify contrasting views of the Community ranging from a tight, ever more integrated economic unit to a looser, wider intergovernmental body based mainly on free trade.

Deepening Versus Widening – Mark II

Prime Minister Major has indicated that a priority of the UK Presidency in the second half of 1992 would be that of widening, eventually to take in Russia. This has been interpreted as reflecting the 'free trade area' approach so strongly advocated by Mrs.Thatcher and has provoked an immediate response from the federalist camp in Brussels warning that the very future of the Community is at stake!

The debate on Widening versus Deepening has regained some of its former momentum as the pressure for accession grows. This centres on the balance between the vast programme of economic and political integration culminating at Maastricht and the growing demand for entry from states which see the evolving European Union as the focus of their search for solutions to political or economic problems and challenges. Commission President Delors has referred to an "objective contradiction" between the Widening and Deepening with particular reference to the institutional aspects of enlargement.

No easy answer exists to this dilemma. But it is convincingly argued, for instance in the 1990 Opinion of the European Parliament, that Deepening and Widening are not necessarily opposed. This view leads on to the conclusion that the appropriate path is that of Deepening and Sequential Widening, pursuing the present integration programme while commencing a phased and coherent strategy of expansion.

The Potential Applicants

Austria and Sweden are recognised as the countries most likely to be in formal entry negotiations before the end of 1992 or early next year. Finland has also applied and may enter into negotiations at the same time.

In his initial response to Maastricht, Austrian Federal Chancellor Vranitsky stated that Austria could support the outcome. He argued that the Common Foreign and Security Policy provisions were acceptable since no country could be compelled to become a member of the WEU and he gave it as his opinion that there appear to be no obstacles to the opening of negotiations this year.

The troublesome issues surrounding the completion of the European Economic Area Treaty have, if anything, accelerated the trend towards full membership as the most acceptable option for the present EFTA states. Next in line may well be Norway where the ruling Labour party will decide its position in the autumn. Both Switzerland and Iceland are now debating possible applications and may move on this issue in the near future.

The potential applicants in Central and Eastern Europe consist of Hungary, Czechoslovakia and Poland and Commission President Delors has stated that they will be ready to become members of the Community at the beginning of the next century. This view is increasingly accepted as realistic. Other potential members whether in the Baltic, the Balkans or the CIS are visible today but are most unlikely to be accepted in the short term. The wide-ranging Association Agreements with a number of these states will take on a special priority.

Turkey is stepping up diplomatic pressure for reconsideration of the 'hold' on its application, in particular since its change of government, while Malta and Cyprus continue to claim serious attention for their formal applications.

The Issues: Institutions

There is widespread recognition of the huge institutional implications of further enlargement. Maastricht did nothing to solve these and left it to the Commission to bring forward relevant proposals at Lisbon. Far-reaching decisions are required, for example, in the areas of decision-making, representation, and balance between institutions and voting.

In the European Parliament some radical ideas have emerged for institutional change in the context of Enlargement: for example, revolving the Council Presidency between the five largest states with the others having vice-presidents only; qualified majority voting on all issues; election of the Commission President by the European Parliament; the Commission to be of a limited number not necessarily one per member state; numbers of MEPs to be fixed in accordance with 'inverse proportionality' giving smaller countries a preferential share of seats; the Parliament to have voting rights on Foreign and Security Policy; and the number of working languages to be limited.

The Commission President has suggested in a French TV interview that, with significant enlargement, the European Council would have a central role "to meet regularly three times a year and to designate, by majority vote, a personality charged with forming the Community Government . . . there will therefore be one person to represent Europe in the areas where this Community is competent, and solely in these areas". More formal Commission views on these issues will be heard in time for the Lisbon European Council and it has been indicated that these will come as "a political, intellectual and institutional shock".

The Issues: Community Budget

It has long been accepted that the current Community Budget does not provide a meaningful basis for the long-term evolution of the EC into a true Union. The Werner, MacDougall, Padoa Schioppa and Delors Reports have all underlined this fact. A recent report prepared for the European Parliament has identified the redistributive requirements of closer integration and puts forward a range of policy alternatives capable

83

of reducing the imbalances and unemployment levels which threaten the attainment of a Union responsive to the needs of all its people.

The work of the Commission reflected in the far-reaching Delors II package is relevant both to the existing needs of the Community and to the Enlargement issue. For, while the net contribution of the EFTA states to the Community Budget would be more significant than the proposed Cohesion Fund in the view of some commentators, the immediate need for assistance to the countries of the East and the longer-term cohesion requirements of a significantly enlarged EC pose great financial challenges. The Lisbon European Council will be faced with far-reaching decisions in this area, with important consequences for Ireland.

The Issues: Economic Considerations

The economic implications of Enlargement differ significantly as between the EFTA member states and other potential applicants. The EFTA states represent, at once, market opportunities and sources of both capital and revenue and should add to the overall economic strength. The others – Turkey, the Central European states and the CIS – are faced by serious economic problems of a structural nature. The solution to these will demand both internal reforms and significant assistance through mechanisms such as Association Agreements and the G-24 Programmes.

The Issues: Political, Security, Defence

The outcome of Maastricht, which strengthens the provisions for Foreign and Security Policy, has deferred the crucial decision on defence policy and structures until 1996. Thus, this issue does not represent an obstacle to entry negotiations for Austria, Sweden and Finland, all of which are neutrals. Their entry at an early stage would bring their special insights and experience to bear on the debate on the 1996 report and on the negotiations which will follow it within the European council. This would be enhanced by the subsequent entry of Switzerland, Cyprus and Malta.

The Central and East European countries and those of the former USSR – both in the Baltics and in the CIS – are now in a potentially unstable and dangerous security vacuum and are most anxious to find a new framework of certainty and cooperation. At the same time, the overall world and European security scene seems certain to change substantially in the years immediately ahead as the dramatic developments since 1989 work themselves out and the evolution of all the security and defence 'actors' including NATO, the WEU, the renascent UN and the CSCE, continues.

Indeed, the Union itself may well be the appropriate focus for the provision of both an acceptable security 'umbrella' and an effective buttress for emerging democratic systems in Central and Eastern Europe. The Community has already successfully played the latter role in the case of the emergence of Greece, Spain and Portugal from fascism in the 1970s.

The Issues: Acquis Communautaire

The Acquis Communautaire which will confront the applicants is considerably enhanced by the outcome of the Maastricht meeting in respect of the EMU project; the Common Foreign and Security Policy and the commitment to consider a common defence policy in 1996. New titles are added to the EEC Treaty and qualified majority voting is provided for in additional policy areas. These, and other, changes must be assessed in the context of the EEA agreement to identify possible problem areas for potential members which will form the major element of the negotiations likely to commence in the second half of the year.

Implications For Ireland

Enlargement has serious implications for this country.

First, this country's attitudes to the long-term vision of the Union and to Ireland's place therein must be addressed, perhaps for the first time.

Second, it will be necessary to respond to the Deepening versus Widening controversy. Ireland requires a position on such issues as the relationship between the pace of Enlargement and the pursuit of further integration, for example, in the political and defence areas. Is Ireland in favour of the evolution of the Community as an 'open' entity capable of offering a secure framework within which new and developing democracies can find a home? Or, is Ireland happy to see the present Twelve, with just a few new members, creating a closed and inward-looking Union concentrating on its own economic and political interests?

Third, serious thought must be given to the Institutional issues which are linked to the controversy between intergovernmentalism and supranationalism, especially as it touches on the role of the Council and of the European Council. The possibility of an emerging 'Directorate' of the larger member states is given credibility by recent ideas circulating in the European Parliament and has been specifically warned against by the Luxembourg Foreign Minister, Jacques Poos. Issues must also be faced in connection with the roles of both Commission and Parliament and their involvement in decision-making. Technical issues such as the number of official languages also require careful consideration not least because they have important political overtones.

Fourth, clarification of Irish policy on security and defence and a real debate on neutrality are urgently necessary in the context of a profoundly changed European political scene, particularly the transformation of the Soviet Union. Concepts such as 'common security' and 'pan-European' security structures must find their way on to the national political agenda. The positive elements of Irish neutrality should be clearly formulated so that we can make a relevant contribution to the evolving Community debate on Defence Policy.

Fifth, for Ireland, Enlargement also has important financial and economic aspects. The entry of the EFTA applicants may be seen as positive in terms of markets, investment and finance for action on Cohesion etc. Further expansion to the East and South may give rise to competition for funds together with threats to certain traditional markets e.g. agriculture. The decisions to be made later this year on the Community Budget and the Cohesion Fund within the framework of the Delors II package will be crucial and will call for a coherent national strategy to promote Ireland's particular interests and to contribute, in a spirit of solidarity, to the interests of other member states.

Conclusion

The Enlargement debate has the potential, for these practical reasons, to stimulate exactly the kind of in-depth examination of the key European questions that was absent from Irish politics before this country benefited from the first expansion of the Community in 1973 and which has been avoided ever since. Given the direct relevance of these questions for our economic and political wellbeing it is to be hoped that the Maastricht Treaty, and its implications in areas such as Enlargement, will prompt the requisite answers.

12. TOWARDS A FEDERAL UNION?

Patrick Keatinge

In trying to understand where the Treaty of Maastricht is leading to, it is necessary to see it as a whole. It is all too easy, in teasing out this or that aspect, to neglect its overall impact or to jump to sweeping conclusions on the basis of inadequate evidence. We argued in Chapter 1 that it was possible to use the *federal model* as a yardstick against which the overall development of any union of states can be measured. A single federal state lies at one end of a spectrum of possibilities, with an amorphous collection of sovereign states at the other. In between are confederations of varying degrees of cohesiveness. In this chapter we ask how far, and in what ways, the Treaty of Maastricht moves its member states towards the federal destination. Do the new policies and processes add up to a qualitatively different political system, or is the European Union no more than the old Community under another name?

Policies For Union?

It was the creation of a customs union which gave credibility to the federal aspirations behind the original EEC, and the completion of the Single Market – the famous '1992 Programme' – renewed that credibility after a long period of drift. The major contribution of Maastricht to this 'federal imperative' is undoubtedly the provision for an eventual single currency. It is a natural corollary of the Single Market, an element of macro-economic stability, and it reinforces the case for a federal political authority. In short, this aspect of EMU is a very significant piece in the federal jigsaw.

It is not, however, the final piece. A federal economy arguably requires a budget of sufficient size to allow for significant redistributive policies, and the achievement of that goal is not guaranteed through the Treaty. On the other hand, it is not excluded, and it might further be argued that the greater emphasis on economic and social cohesion in the document at least edges the Union in the direction of an eventual federal budget. However, there are likely to be many political battles on that front before the outcome is clear.

The Treaty also expands the policy scope in other fields, by giving the Union a new role (or reinforcing existing activities) alongside the national governments. This can be seen as part of the quest for an agreed division of labour between the Union and its members – a necessary element in the creation of a federal state – but it also identifies the inner core of the national state. Is the federal glass half full or half empty? The curious saga of the protocol on social policy illustrates the difficulty of making firm judgements. Taken at face value, the United Kingdom's opting out *now* (as well as potentially in the EMU context) creates a two-tier system which threatens to delay an eventual economic union. Yet it may in time prove to be no more than just another unscheduled halt on Westminster's long march to Europe.

So far as the policy content of the common foreign and security policy is concerned, the Treaty is evolutionary rather than revolutionary; it is the actual revolution in world politics since 1989 rather than the Treaty itself which is likely to be the determining factor. Supporters of a federal Europe argue that the consequent instability highlights the need for a coherent (i.e. federal) response, yet history shows that crises can break as well as make federal unions. Defence – a necessary though not sufficient element of a federal union – is in the text as an explicit aspiration, but the Treaty does not include a commitment to a common defence policy now. Likewise, cooperation on judicial and home affairs starts with the codification of existing practice, and although it contains the potential for significant joint action, this type of policy is kept at arm's length from the would-be federal core of the Union.

Does the inclusion of the principle of subsidiarity represent 'federalism – by – stealth'? It would seem to allow the Union to develop policies when national governments manifestly fail to provide effective policies at the national level. However, national governments are often adept at turning a blind eye to their deficiencies, and the onus of proof seems in any case to be on the Commission, and eventually the European Court of Justice. Subsidiarity will no doubt provide much of the currency of bargaining in the years to come, but its presence will not of itself clinch a federal deal.

Is it in Ireland's interests that the Union's policies be more or less federal in character? In order to maximise the advantages of further economic integration, but at the same time reduce the vulnerability of a small peripheral economy, it can be argued the federal route has distinct advantages, particularly in its budgetary capacity. In this view the Treaty of Maastricht may not go far enough, or fast enough. There may be doubts about its capacity to provide effective management for an *economic*, not just a monetary, union; only a truly federal budget can hope to achieve the redistributive target at which cohesion is aimed.

The price of more economic federalism is not restricted to a further loss of national economic instruments. The case for federal control of foreign and security policy, including defence, may also be strengthened by moving in this direction. Given traditional Irish reservations on the latter point, the balance of advantage is less clear-cut. The power to decide between peace and war is sometimes seen as the essence of national independence. In fact that position has been conceded by many modern states, without federalism being an issue.

These countries have long been accustomed to military commitments inside confederations; their essential concern is their capacity to influence the policy of the alliance to which they belong. From the point of view of a small state in an alliance, the critical point is that its larger partners should also be constrained by alliance commitments, which would not be the case in a world without such commitments. Considerations of this sort, however, bring us to the changes in the policy process which are contained in the Treaty of Maastricht.

Process For Union?

The structure of the Treaty makes it plain that there will be no federal union at this stage. The European Union is still a confederation, if a very complex and far-reaching one. The separate pillars reflect its hybrid nature; the Community pillar is closest to the federal model, the foreign and security policy pillar contains only a hint of the federal aspiration, and there is none in the judicial and home affairs pillar. Judicial review, an essential component of a federal system, only applies to the first pillar.

The changes to the institutions and their policymaking procedures also confirm the mixture between the federal or supranational approach and intergovernmentalism, with its emphasis on the primacy of the member states. The extension of qualified majority voting, the partial expansion in the Parliament's role, the enhanced presence of the Commission, the emphasis on common citizenship – all of these may be seen as moves in a federal direction. So, too, are the institutional arrangements for the final stage of the Economic and Monetary Union. On the other hand, the position of the European Council, in its present form the quintessence of intergovernmental decision-making, is also underlined, and the convoluted experiment of 'joint action' in the second and third pillars only serves to demonstrate the resistance to federal policy-making in these fields.

A very striking feature of the new European Union is the sheer complexity of its decision-making procedures. The variety of legal bases and different procedural rules clearly worries those politicians and officials who will have to make them work. This is a far cry from the requirement in a federal state for a clear distribution of political authority. There may be negative consequences for the efficacy of the policy-making system, in the form of disputes between the institutions, and delays in the process of legislation and implementation. Complexity certainly detracts from the transparency of the political process, and hence from the requirements of democratic accountability.

It is perhaps not surprising that there is some ambivalence in the views which have been expressed on where Ireland's interests lie in this regard. On the one hand, a small state has an obvious interest in a policy-making system which is ordered by rules rather than the vagaries of arbitrary power, exercised by larger neighbours. The Commission, along with the European Court of Justice a guarantor of these rules, is thus a natural ally in this context. But so long as we are accustomed to think of Ireland as a *state* – as well as a society – we tend to focus on the national government's representation in those institutions which are composed of states. Thus we rely on the Council of Ministers and the European Council as the arenas in which our interests are protected. The promotion of Irish interests, and accountability in general, through the European Parliament is correspondingly neglected.

Moving to a federal system could push this ambivalence to breaking point. In a federal system the Irish 'state' would become a political unit in which some sort of 'home rule' would be exercised. That might meet the interests of Ireland as a society, but it would be a fundamental change for the people whose job it is to run the existing, and still formally sovereign, Irish state. Of course, this prospect faces each and every member state represented at Maastricht, which may be one reason why the Treaty did not attain the federal nirvana.

However, the signatories did not regard their work as expressing the last word in the institutional development of the Union. On the contrary, it contains a commitment to convene a further Inter Governmental Conference in 1996. Does that imply that we are locked in to an 'irreversible' process in a federal direction, or was it merely a device to save the existing level of agreement by postponing the intractable elements of the negotiations?

'1996 And All That'

Integration has always been marked by the discipline of the deadline. It has not always worked – European Union was originally scheduled for 1980! – but since the Single European Act it can be taken as a reasonably serious indicator of political intent. The choice of 1996 was partly influenced by the possibility of reviewing the fifty-year WEU Treaty in 1998; partly it reflects an implicit cyclical pattern of 'medium-term reviews'. It is also an important point of decision in the EMU timetable. It will be faced by a new Commission and a new European Parliament. That much we know about 1996.

Nevertheless, it is four years away from the previous 'mythical year' – 1992 – and if we consider the extent of change which occurred during the four years before that, the perils of political prediction are plain to see. The situation in and around Russia, and the consequent response of major world powers and particularly the United States can hardly be guessed at. Even in the more stable environment of domestic politics, 1996 lies beyond the next general election.

It also lies beyond the stage where the existing members of the European Union will have been confronted by the central political challenge of enlargement. Austria, Sweden, Finland, and maybe others could be full members by then. Former Eastern bloc countries will be pressing their claims more convincingly.This will provide a most acute test of the viability of the institutional framework agreed at Maastricht. Can the relative intimacy of a club of twelve be sustained in one of twenty? If the greater numbers and diversity between the members is not to bring the policymaking machinery to a stop, will there not be a need for a much more radical reform than the present one?

One answer in the intergovernmental mould might be the creation of an 'executive committee', but this would probably enhance the power of the larger states. From the point of view of the smaller members, in these circumstances the supranational option might seem more attractive. To accept majority voting as the rule, perhaps even in sensitive areas such as foreign and security policy, might be the only way both to maintain the capacity to act and to avoid a 'great power' directorate. In other words, the fundamental issues which appear to have been put off to 1996 may well call for decision before then, simply because of the pressures of enlargement.

While it is probable that the pressures to make some sort of change will continue to be strong, we cannot be certain of the direction the Union might take. It is possible to envisage a scenario where the integrative elements of the Treaty of Maastricht proceed as planned, and the next Inter Governmental Conference, whether in 1996 or before, does in fact lead to the federal threshold. Yet it is equally plausible to assume a degree of slippage, or even of failure to achieve the designated goals. The EMU convergence criteria may prove unrealisable, the USA may wish to continue its role as military leader of a European alliance, or particular member states may backtrack on existing commitments. In such circumstances the European Union might merely mark time, develop into a two-tier form of confederation, or even unravel altogether.

Neither of these contrasting scenarios, nor any variations of them, can be predicted with any degree of confidence from the vantage point of 1992. It is not inconceivable that a quite new form of union could emerge over the next few years, in response to a combination of unforeseen events. The European Union will be what we make it.

European Union

The Treaty of Maastricht undeniably contains important changes to the process of European integration. It builds on the completion of the Single Market, which was the focus of the previous exercise in deepening integration. It stakes claims on a broader front than the Single European Act, and raises the prospect of a federal Europe in a way we have not seen since Ireland first applied for membership more than thirty years ago.

However, the Treaty does not create a federal union. Nor does it achieve the level of integration which the advocates of federalism would regard as the penultimate stage, the threshold of a federal Europe. To that extent, purists may carp at the attribution of the term 'union' to the rather lop-sided outcome of the negotiations. Nevertheless, if the Treaty is ratified, the European Union will be a political reality, not just rhetoric.

The European Union is about changing an existing confederation into a higher gear. Already doubts have been expressed whether the gear is high enough, not just with regard to federal aspirations, but simply in order to face the many challenges on the European agenda. If Maastricht cannot provide an ordered framework for the future, it is hard to see what will. A renationalisation of European politics cannot be ruled out as a likely alternative. At best this would mean trying to pursue the general goals of the Treaty in an even less coordinated way; at worst it might lead to a fragmentation of Europe, and the emergence of unconstrained rivalries between the larger states.

THE TREATY AND THE CONSTITUTION

13. THE LEGAL AND CONSTITUTIONAL IMPLICATIONS

Gerard Hogan and Niamh Hyland

We now turn to consider some of the more specifically Irish dimensions of the ratification process. The object of this particular chapter is to chart some of the various legal and constitutional dimensions that would seem to arise now that Ireland is confronted with the choice of whether to ratify the Maastricht Treaty. We first consider the necessity for a referendum in view of the Supreme Court's decision in *Crotty v An Taoiseach*. We next consider the legal consequences of non-ratification, should that occur, in the context of proceeding to examine in brief outline some of the more important substantive changes to be effected by the Treaty. Finally, we examine whether – as has been claimed in some quarters – this will be the last opportunity for a referendum before the final disappearance of Irish neutrality.

The Need For A Referendum

Article 29.4.3 of the Constitution allows the State to join the European Community and confers constitutional immunity on all measures which are "necessitated" by virtue of that membership. This provision was inserted by the Third Amendment of the Constitution Act 1972 following a referendum in June 1972. It was further amended by the Tenth Amendment of the Constitution Act 1987, which, again following a referendum in May 1987, allowed the State to ratify the Single European Act (SEA). What is clear is that while Article 29.4.3 contemplates an emerging and evolving Community, there are nonetheless limits to the extent to which the Treaty of Rome can be amended without further recourse to the people by way of referendum.

This principle emerges from the decision of the Supreme Court in

Crotty v An Taoiseach [1987] IR 713. Here the plaintiff had challenged the constitutionality of the Single European Act on the ground that this Act went beyond the essential scope or objective of the Communities as established in 1957 and, hence, that the SEA was not within the scope of the amendment. The SEA itself was divided into two main parts, Title II and Title III. Title II conferred additional powers on the Community institutions to ensure that progress was made towards completion of the Single Market. This was largely effected by the introduction of majority voting at Council level. The Supreme Court saw no objection to the provisions of Title II:

> *The Community was thus a developing organism with diverse and changing methods for making decisions and an inbuilt and clearly expressed objective of expansion and progress, both in terms of the number of member states and in terms of the mechanics to be used in the achievement of its agreed objectives. Having regard to these considerations, it is the opinion of the Court that neither the proposed changes from unanimity to qualified majority, nor the identification of topics which, while not separately stated, are within the original aims and objectives of the European Community, bring these amendments outside the scope of the authorisation contained in Article 29.4.3.*

A majority of the Court went on, nonetheless, to hold that the provisions of Title III of the SEA (which provided more formal rules for European Political Cooperation) violated the foregoing principle, inasmuch as they provided for a political dimension to the Community not previously envisaged. The application of this principle in the case of Title III (which was a rather innocuous attempt to put foreign policy cooperation on a more formal and legalistic footing) may be questioned, but there can be no doubt that, in the light of *Crotty v An Taoiseach,* this is the test which will now have to be followed.

Judged by this test, there can be no question but that adherence by this State to the Maastricht Treaty would require a further constitutional amendment. The establishment, for example, of a monetary union goes far beyond anything the EC has hitherto attempted and has profound implications for national sovereignty. Such a profound and radical change in the nature and structure of the Community can only be effected – as far as this State is concerned – via a referendum.

It may be noted that only two of the twelve states propose to submit ratification of the Treaty to a referendum, namely, Denmark and Ireland.

This of itself is nothing unusual, since Article R of the Treaty of Maastricht provides that the Treaty "shall be ratified by the High Contracting Parties in accordance with their respective constitutional requirements" (a similar provision may be found in Article 236 of the Treaty of Rome). In the case of Denmark and Ireland, this requires a referendum and in the case of the other member states, legislation alone is all that has been deemed to be necessary.

Legal Consequences of non-Ratification by Ireland of the Treaty on European Union and the Possibility of two-tiered Membership

Any amendments to the EEC Treaty must be made under Article 236 of that Treaty. Article 236 states that the amendments shall be determined "by common accord" by representatives of the governments of member states. After agreement on the amendments has been reached, they shall enter into force "after being ratified by all the Member States in accordance with their respective constitutional requirements".

Thus the short answer to the consequence of non-ratification by Ireland is that the existing Treaty on European Union could not enter into force *at all* as the requirements of Article 236 would not have been met.

However, it is unlikely that the rest of the Community would allow Ireland to halt the tide of integration in this way. What action could the Community take to proceed with European Union should Ireland decide not to ratify the Treaty?

The most draconian action would be to force Ireland to leave the Community altogether. The EEC Treaty does not contain any provisions for withdrawal from the Community and to date no member state has left (although Greenland which was in the Community due to its association with Denmark did leave following a referendum in 1985).

Therefore it is hard to predict the kind of rights and obligations that the Community would impose on a member state which decided to leave. Obviously a decision to leave the Community altogether would have very serious implications for Ireland which will not be discussed here.

The other alternative the Community might have would be to devise a system of 'two-tiered' membership, whereby Ireland and any other member state who chose not to progress further with European Union would remain in the existing Community and the rest of the member states would form a new 'European Union'.

Is this system of two-tiered membership viable? This is an important question because if Ireland does not ratify the Treaty on European Union it may be the only alternative to leaving the Community.

If two-tiered membership is a viable alternative, what would the legal implications be for Ireland? Could Ireland remain a functional member of the Community?

Obviously it is impossible to answer these questions definitively; all that is attempted here is (a) a teasing out of the legal consequences of two-tiered membership and (b) an assessment of the legality of two-tiered membership. For the purposes of (a) it is assumed that two-tiered membership would involve a re-negotiation of a Treaty essentially similar to the present one on European Union. However it must be borne in mind that if two-tiered membership becomes a reality the present Treaty on European Union would have to be completely re-negotiated and therefore it is impossible to predict with any certainty what the consequences would be for Ireland of two-tiered membership.

Both the institutional and substantive provisions of the present Treaty on European Union will be examined, and the effect of Ireland deciding not to participate in the Treaty will be assessed.

Institutional Provisions

The new Treaty has made significant changes in the legislative procedure both at Parliament and Council level.

It introduces a co-decision making power whereby the Council and the Parliament jointly make legislative decisions, and it extends the areas where the cooperation procedure and the assent procedure are applicable. It also extends legislative competence to new areas which were not previously within EC competence.

If a system of two-tiered membership was introduced, whereby a new treaty which resembles the present one was signed by all member states except Ireland, what would be the position of Ireland in relation to the above changes in the legislative process?

There are two questions inherent in this – first, whether Ireland could participate in the legislative process, and second, if not, what status would legislation enacted under the new procedures have in Ireland.

Participation In The Legislative Process

The member states have a significant input into the legislative process at two levels – Parliament and Council.

Obviously the amount of influence that Parliament has over legislation will depend on the type of legislative procedure that is being employed. However the co-decision procedure, the cooperation procedure and the assent procedure all involve a real exercise of power by the Parliament. If Ireland failed to sign the new Treaty, it is probable that no Irish MEPs could participate in any voting procedures which derived from the Treaty. This would seem to be true both from the point of view of EEC law and from the point of view of Irish law.

In relation to EEC law it is hard to see how the Irish MEPs could participate in a voting procedure laid down by a Treaty which their member state – Ireland – had not signed. It is true of course that MEPs are not representatives of their member state in the same way as Council members but nonetheless their legitimacy in the Parliament derives from the fact that they are representing the people of Ireland.

In relation to Irish law, the MEPs would have no authorisation to participate in the voting procedure as the Irish people, by rejecting the Treaty in a constitutional referendum, would have clearly indicated that they did not wish to transfer any further sovereignty to the EC, which would include, *inter alia*, giving the Parliament increased legislative powers.

At the Council level many of the same arguments against Irish participation apply. It is unlikely the Irish representative at the Council of Ministers could be considered to have the right to participate in voting mechanisms laid down by any new Treaty if Ireland was not a signatory. This is because a party who is not a signatory to an agreement is not usually able to participate in decisions arrived at using structures set up by that agreement.

This point of view is supported by the Protocol on Social Policy which has been signed by all of the member states with the exception of the UK. It states "The UK shall not take part in the deliberations and the adoption by the Council of Commission proposals made on the basis of this Protocol". This Protocol lays down the voting procedure to be followed, which excludes the UK. Legislation adopted under the qualified majority procedure will require 44 votes instead of the usual 54 votes. Legislation which must be passed unanimously requires all member states, save for the UK, to vote in favour.

In relation to Irish law, the Irish member of the Council could not be considered to be endowed with the necessary authority from the Irish people to participate in the enactment of legislation under the new procedures. This is particularly true in relation to the enactment of legislation in areas which were not previously within the ambit of the EEC Treaty such as culture, public health and consumer protection. The Irish people, by deciding not to ratify the Treaty on European Union, would clearly be indicating that, *inter alia,* they did not want Ireland to hand over sovereignty to the Community in any new areas.

Impact Of Legislation Adopted Under The New Treaty In Ireland

Given that the above assumptions are correct, any legislative measures which are adopted under the procedures established by the new Treaty would have to be adopted without Irish participation.

The corollary to this would seem to be that such legislation could not be applicable to Ireland. Again this assertion is supported by the Protocol on Social Policy which states "By way of derogation to the Treaty, the Community acts thus adopted by the Council . . . shall not be applicable to the UK".

At present EEC law is applicable in Ireland by virtue of Article 189 of the EEC Treaty, by virtue of implementing national legislation and by virtue of the twin doctrines of direct effect and supremacy which have been developed over the years by the European Court of Justice.

No matter which of these methods is used to ensure the applicability of EEC law in Ireland, they all assume that Ireland has participated in the enactment of the relevant EEC legislation. The promise of such participation is the basis on which the member states agreed to transfer their sovereignty to the Community in certain areas. It is this transferral of sovereignty which gives Community law its legitimacy. Thus if Ireland did not participate in the enactment of Community legislation, the legislation could not be deemed to be legitimately enacted in relation to Ireland and therefore it would not be applicable to Ireland.

It seems likely the Court of Justice would endorse this approach. In a recent Opinion of the Court regarding the constitutionality of the agreement creating the European Economic Area (EEA) , discussed in more detail below, the Court found the agreement to be incompatible with the Treaty of Rome on the ground that it was incompatible both with Article 164 of the Treaty which states that "The Court of Justice shall ensure that in the interpretation and application of this Treaty the law is observed" and incompatible with "the very foundations of the Community".

It is submitted that any attempt to make legislation, enacted without the participation of Ireland, enforceable in Ireland, would be a failure to observe the "law" referred to in Article 164 and would be incompatible with the foundations of the Community.

From the Irish point of view it is unlikely that legislation enacted in this way would benefit from the immunity from constitutional challenge ordinarily conferred by Article 29.4.3 of the Irish Constitution. This Article provides that no provision of EEC law can be challenged against the provisions of the Irish Constitution if the laws, measures, or acts are "necessitated by the obligations of membership of the Communities".

It is inconceivable that an Irish court would decide that a law was "necessitated by the obligations of membership of the Communities" and would protect that law from constitutional challenge where Irish MEPs and the Irish Council member had refused to participate in the enactment of that law due to a perceived lack of authority. Thus if the above analysis is correct no legislation enacted under the new Treaty will be applicable to Ireland.

How significant is this likely to be in practice? Obviously this is impossible to predict accurately as it will depend on the type of legislation enacted under the new procedures. However, the majority of legislation adopted in future is likely to be adopted under the new Treaty procedures, since the new legislative processes encompass almost all significant areas in the Treaty.

To focus on one particular area, all legislation on the freedom of movement for workers and much of the legislation on freedom of establishment, including directives on the mutual recognition of diplomas, certificates and other formal qualifications, will be decided under Article 189B – the co-decision procedure. Thus, to take a very simple example, a directive which enabled the diplomas of interior decorators to be recognised throughout the European Community would not be applicable in Ireland and therefore Ireland would not be obliged to recognise the diplomas of non-Irish interior decorators.

Very importantly, all measures which have as their object the establishment and functioning of the Single Market will be adopted under Article 189B. Thus Ireland would be excluded from any future measures relating to the Single Market.

Furthermore, all legislation in new areas of competence would be inapplicable in Ireland. This would have a dual effect. Within Ireland, Irish citizens could not rely on any Community legislation in these new areas of competence and therefore the aims of the various pieces of legislation would not be realised in Ireland.

Outside Ireland the consequences could be equally serious. If new Community rules did not apply in Ireland other member states might possibly decide not to extend the benefit of these rules to Irish goods, services, or people which were in circulation in the remainder of the Community. Thus Ireland's position within the Community could be seriously jeopardised.

Substantive Provisions

In other areas apart from the legislative one, Ireland's non-participation in a Treaty on European Union would create serious problems. Obviously all these areas cannot be gone into in detail but a few of the more obvious examples are highlighted:

Citizenship   The new Treaty creates European citizenship, which formally gives EC citizens the right to live and work anywhere in the Community and to vote in European and local elections wherever they live. If Ireland failed to sign a Treaty on European Union Irish citizens could not become 'European citizens'. This would result in the creation of a two-tiered body of Europeans: those who could become citizens and those who could not.

Economic and Social Cohesion   If Ireland failed to sign a new Treaty it could be perceived to be opting out of the onerous obligations imposed by the Treaty. If this was the case it is most unlikely that it would be permitted to benefit from the advantages which are likely to accrue from the Treaty, in particular a significant increase in Structural Funds.

Twin Pillars Both in relation to Title V – the provisions on a Common Foreign and Security Policy – and in relation to Title VI – the provisions on Cooperation in the spheres of Justice and Home Affairs – it is hard to estimate the consequences of non-participation as it is unclear how they will operate in practice.

The most obvious consequence for Ireland in the field of Foreign Policy is that Ireland would be completely marginalised and would have no input on any decisions or actions taken in the area.

In the area of Cooperation in the spheres of Justice and Home Affairs the member states agree to a system of intergovernmental cooperation and joint action in a variety of matters in the field of crime and movement of non-Community nationals. Thus Ireland would be excluded from this system of cooperation and joint action in the above areas. Obviously this would have disadvantages for Ireland in attempting to control crime, particularly international crime and it would also create serious problems in relation to the movement of third country nationals within Ireland.

Of course Ireland would still be free to forge individual links with other member states to foster cooperation in the above areas – Article K.7 of Title VI states that "the provisions of this Title shall not prevent the establishing or developing of closer cooperation between two or more member states to the extent that such cooperation does not conflict with or impede with that provided for in this Title". However the member states' freedom to conclude bilateral agreements in this area would obviously be significantly impeded and it is doubtful if Ireland could conclude useful agreements in this area after a new Treaty was signed, even assuming the political willingness to do so on the part of the remaining member states existed.

The most intransigent problem seems to be that which concerns legislation. If the majority of new EC legislation is inapplicable to, and in Ireland, Ireland would very quickly become a member of the Community in name only. Obviously existing EC legislation will still be applicable in Ireland but this will rapidly become out of date as it is replaced by new legislation under a new Treaty.

The Legality Of Two-Tiered Membership
It has been assumed throughout that it would be legally possible to create

two-tiered membership of the Community. However it is by no means certain that a structure could be created that would be acceptable to the Court of Justice.

There seems to be two possible ways to create two-tiered membership – (i) by amending the existing EEC Treaty under Article 236 to provide for two-tiered membership, which would necessitate the agreement of all the existing member states, and (ii) by creating a whole new supranational organisation which would run side by side with the existing EC. This would probably not necessitate the agreement of all the existing member states, only those who were party to the new organisation.

(i) In relation to the first option it is possible that the Court of Justice might find that two-tiered membership breaches fundamental principles of EC law and therefore is incompatible with the EEC Treaty itself. For example, under Article 2 of the EEC Treaty the Community shall "progressively approximate the economic policies of member states". It is hard to see how this could be reconciled with two-tiered membership, assuming that the second tier of member states went ahead with EMU. This is only one example: many others can be found in the EEC Treaty as it exists at present. Of course, theoretically it is possible for the EEC Treaty to be so fundamentally amended under Article 236 that two-tiered membership would not breach any principles of EC law under the new amended structure. However this may not be possible: in the EEA Opinion the Court of Justice held that the amendment of an article of the EEC Treaty could not cure a proposed association agreement of its illegality where the agreement conflicted with the very foundations of the Community. Thus if two-tiered membership system was deemed to conflict with the very foundations of the Community, there could be no acceptable amendment of the EEC Treaty. In that case the only remaining option would be to scrap the whole EEC Treaty and start again – a daunting prospect!

(ii) In relation to the second option – the creation of a separate new supranational organisation – the legality of the arrangement would differ depending on whether the new organisation utilised existing EC institutional structures or not. In both cases the Opinion of the Court of Justice concerning the constitutionality of the agreement creating the EEA (Opinion 1/91), referred to above, proves most illuminating.

In this Opinion, the Court was examining the legality of the association agreement between the EC and the EFTA countries whereby a European Economic Area would be established. Two provisions of the agreement in particular were examined – that which established an EEA court which would have jurisdiction to settle disputes between the contracting parties, and that which gave a court or tribunal of an EFTA state the option of referring a case to the Court of Justice in certain circumstances. Thus the legality of two acts was under review; the establishment of a new institution – the EEA court – and the use by the new structure of an existing Community institution – the Court of Justice.

The decision of the Court with regard to the establishment of the EEA court seems to show that the conclusion of an agreement establishing a new organisation with its own institutions would breach EC law, at least insofar as the organisation and its institutions claimed competence in areas which are within the exclusive jurisdiction of the EC at present.

In the Opinion of the Court, giving the EEA court jurisdiction was held to conflict with "Article 164 of the Treaty of Rome and more generally, with the very foundations of the Community", essentially because it meant that the EEA court would be ruling on matters which already came under the jurisdiction of the EC, e.g. free movement and competition. As a result both the Court of Justice and the EEA court would, independently of each other, have had jurisdiction to decide matters which up until the agreement had been wholly governed by EC law. The Court of Justice stated that "... it follows that the jurisdiction conferred on the EEA court is likely to adversely affect the allocation of responsibilities defined in the Treaties and hence the autonomy of the Community legal order".

If a new supranational organisation of the type discussed above was set up with its own institutions, these institutions would almost certainly be operating in areas where EC institutions operate at present. This would seem be incompatible with the "foundations of the Community" and thus any member state of the EC which became a party to such a supranational organisation would almost certainly be in breach of its obligations under Community law.

If the new supranational organisation attempted to utilise the existing institutions and structures of the EC, its compatibility with EC law would depend on how the relationship was structured. In the above mentioned Opinion, the Court of Justice held that provision which gave a court or tribunal of an EFTA state the option of referring a case to the Court of

Justice was incompatible with Community law as it utilised the Court of Justice in a way impermissible under the Community legal system. Thus the use of the Community institutions would have to be in accordance with the Treaty. The use by another supranational organisation of Community institutions would almost certainly necessitate amendment of the EEC Treaty under Article 236 and therefore the agreement of all the member states would be required.

It is obvious from the foregoing that there are many legal obstacles to the establishment of two-tiered membership. Apart altogether from the legal difficulties it should also be remembered that such an approach may not be politically acceptable within the EC.

To use a well worn analogy, the Community is a moving train, and the choice may well be between jumping fully on the train or disembarking altogether.

The Last Opportunity For A Referendum?

Finally, we must consider the question of whether this is the last opportunity for a referendum before the disappearance of the twelve nation states and the creation of a European Federal State. As Patrick Keatinge has pointed out in Chapter 1, even the use of the term "European Union" is something of a misnomer. As he points out, the very term "Union" had previously been reserved by advocates of a federal Europe for "a very advanced form of confederation, so advanced as to be on the threshold of transformation into a federal state".

While the Maastricht Treaty undoubtedly advances the cause of further European integration, it does not by any standards create the form of European Union that will lead to the disappearance of the individual nation states. In fact, it may not be unfair to the Maastricht Treaty to regard it as a more elaborate version of the Single European Act: in other words, effecting far-reaching amendments to existing Community law, but not yet creating a European federal state.

Apart from the fact that the integrity of the existing nation states is expressly recognised by the Treaty, it is also clear from the Treaty that Ireland's military neutrality has not, as yet, been wholly undermined. It is true that Article J establishes a "common foreign and security policy", but this is qualified by the provisions of Article J.4.1 which envisages the eventual framing of a "common defence policy, which might in time lead to a common defence", i.e., implying that such a policy does not as yet exist and can only be created by further Treaty amendment. This is further qualified in the case of Ireland by the provisions of Article J.4.4:

> *The policy of the Union in accordance with this Article shall not prejudice the specific character of the security and defence policy of certain Member States...*

All of this means that, if Ireland's military neutrality is ultimately to be abandoned with the concomitant creation of a common defence policy and common defence structures within the Union, then this in turn will require further amendment to the Treaty of Maastricht. The very possibility of such an amendment is envisaged by Article N.2 of Treaty of Maastricht, which provides for a new conference of the representatives of the Member States in 1996 "to examine those provisions of this Treaty for which revision is provided". This, of course, includes defence and security policy. Ireland's concurrence and ratification of this amendment will not only be necessary, but a further constitutional amendment and referendum will be required before this could come about.

14. PROTOCOL 17

Gerard Hogan

In the light of the controversy concerning the decision of the High Court and Supreme Court in *Attorney General v X* – which dominated both Irish (and, to a lesser extent, European) politics in the months of February and March 1992 – the question of the Abortion Protocol to the Maastricht Treaty has assumed particular importance. Since the proper interpretation of both Article 40.3.3 of the Constitution and the terms of the Protocol itself are crucial to this debate, it may be helpful at this stage to set them out in full. Article 40.3.3 provides that:

> *The State acknowledges the right to life of the unborn and, with due regard to the equal right to life of the mother, guarantees in its laws to respect, and, as far as practicable, by its laws to defend and vindicate that right.*

Protocol No. 17 to the Maastricht Treaty states that:

> *Nothing in the Treaty on European Union or in the Treaties establishing the European Communities, or in the Treaties or Acts modifying or supplementing those Treaties, shall affect <u>the application in Ireland</u> of Article 40.3.3 of the Constitution of Ireland.*

It may be noted in passing that much of the present controversy centres on the proper interpretation to be given to the underlined words.

The most recent origins of the controversy may be traced to the decision of the European Court of Justice (ECJ) in Luxembourg in *SPUC v Grogan* (C-159/90) in September 1991. In this case, certain student organisations sought the right to distribute information which would have provided the identity and location of certain clinics in England where abortions are performed. The Supreme Court granted (see [1989] IR 753) an interlocutory injunction restraining the distribution of such information, with Finlay C.J. stating clearly that the distribution of such information was a manifest breach of Article 40.3.3:

> *I reject as unsound the contention that the activity involved in this case of publishing in the students' manuals the name, address and telephone number, when telephoned from this State, of abortion clinics in the United Kingdom, and distributing such manuals in Ireland, can be distinguished from the activity condemned by this Court in AG (SPUC) v OPEN DOOR COUNSELLING (1988) IR 593 on the grounds that the facts of that case were that the information was conveyed during periods of one to one non-directive counselling. It is clearly the fact that such information is conveyed to pregnant women, and not the method of communication which creates the unconstitutional illegality and the judgment of this Court in the Open Door Counselling case is not open to any other interpretation.*

It must be stressed, however, that the Supreme Court did not make any final order in the Grogan case, because in the High Court, Carroll J. had referred certain questions of Community law arising out of this case to the Court of Justice in Luxembourg. (The Supreme Court, however, granted an interlocutory injunction restraining the distribution of the information pending the decision of the ECJ and, in the wake of that decision last September, the case will come back shortly before the High Court.)

The ECJ had previously ruled in *Luisi & Carbone v Ministero del Tesoro* [Joined Cases 286/82 and 26/83 (1984) ECR 377] that medical treatment constituted a "service" within the meaning of Article 59 and 60 of the Treaty of Rome, so that potential recipients (as well as providers of a service) had, *prima facie,* a right to travel elsewhere within the Community to receive (or, as the case may be, to provide) those services. Carroll J. had effectively asked the ECJ to rule on whether abortion constituted a "service" within the meaning of the earlier decision in Luisi and, if so, whether the students had the right under Community law to inform Irish women of their right to travel abroad to receive that service.

Answering this first question, the ECJ held that abortion could constitute a service within the meaning of Article 60. The Court dealt with this point by saying:

SPUC, however, maintains that the provision of abortion cannot be regarded as a service on the grounds that it is grossly immoral and involves the destruction of the life of a human being, namely, the unborn child.

Whatever the merits of those arguments on the moral plane, they cannot influence the answer of the national court's first question. It is not for the Court to substitute its assessment for that of the legislature in those Member States where the activities in question are practised legally. Consequently, the answer to the (High Court's) first question must be that medical termination of pregnancy, performed in accordance with the law of the State in which it is carried out constitutes a service within the meaning of Article 60.

The converse of this, of course, is that if other legal systems within the Community did not provide for the provision of lawful abortion, abortion would no longer be regarded as a "service" in the Community law sense (i.e. within the meaning of Article 60 of the Treaty of Rome).

However, the ECJ ruled against the students on the second question, essentially because it was held that they lacked the standing necessary to assert the Community rights which the UK clinics might potentially have had:

The information (in question) is not distributed on behalf of an economic operator established in another Member State. On the contrary, the information constitutes a manifestation of freedom of expression and of the freedom to impart and receive information which is independent of the economic activity carried on by clinics established in another Member State.

The obvious inference here is that had the information been distributed "on behalf of an economic operator established in another Member State" (such as advertisements issued on behalf of English clinics) the result might well have been different. Were the ECJ to find in favour of the clinics in such a case, that decision would, to that extent, automatically override Article 40.3.3 under the present state of Community law. It seems clear that the Protocol was drafted to avoid this very possibility. The Government presumably hoped that, by inserting the Protocol, it could appease the various interest groups who might otherwise have campaigned against the Maastricht Treaty on the ground that European law was in danger of over-riding the provisions of Article 40.3.3.

At all events, this entire question was greatly complicated by the case of *Attorney-General v X*. In this case, the Attorney General sought an injunction to restrain a fourteen-year-old rape victim from leaving the State and thus to prevent her from having an abortion in England. In the High Court, Costello J. granted the injunction, saying, *inter alia,* that the provisions of Article 40.3.3 required the courts, where necessary, to grant an injunction to restrain the right to travel abroad, as otherwise the guarantee with regard to the unborn might be rendered worthless. He accepted that, under Community law, there was a *prima facie* right to travel abroad to obtain an abortion where that service (in the Community law sense of that term) was available in another member state, but held that that right must yield to Irish domestic public policy.

There is, we feel, general agreement among commentators that Costello J's analysis of the domestic public policy issue was questionable, especially bearing in mind that, in the Grogan case, Advocate-General Van Gerven had said that such a ban on travel abroad would not be a proportionate invocation of the domestic public policy exception, so that any such travel ban would have been invalid as a matter of Community law.

While the Supreme Court vacated the injunction, granted by Costello J. they did not, however, rest their judgement on the basis of Community law. As is by now well known, a majority of the Court (Finlay C.J., McCarthy, O'Flaherty and Egan JJ.) held that, as there was in the circumstances of the case, a real and substantial risk to the life of the mother (who was apparently suicidal), that must take precedence over the right to life of the unborn child. As any termination of the pregnancy in those circumstances would have been lawful if performed in Ireland, the travel ban could not be sustained, as there could be no objection to travelling abroad to perform an act which, in the circumstances, would have been lawful if performed in this State.

However, a differently composed majority (consisting of Finlay C.J., Hederman and Egan JJ.) held that , as a matter of *Irish constitutional law,* it might still be necessary and appropriate *in some other circumstances* to grant an injunction to restrain a mother from leaving Ireland where she was seeking to have an abortion in another country. The attitude of Egan J. in this respect may be regarded as representative of this particular majority:

> *The right to travel can only effectively arise in reference to an intention to procure an unlawful abortion and must surely rank*

lower than the right to life of the unborn. It may well be that proof of an intention to commit an unlawful act cannot amount to an offence, but I am dealing here with the question of an unborn child within the jurisdiction being removed from the jurisdiction with the stated intention of depriving it of its right to life. In face of a positive obligation to defend and vindicate such a right it cannot reasonably be argued that such a right to travel simpliciter can take precedence over such a right. (I again emphasise that that the question of European Community law is not being considered).

It may well be that instances of a declared intention and proof of such would be very rare indeed and there is also the position that the supervision of a court order would be difficult, but these considerations must, in my opinion, yield precedence to the defence and vindication of the right to life.

It is clear, therefore, that the Supreme Court has held that, in appropriate cases, the right to travel must yield to the right to life of the unborn. In other words, in cases where the abortion would not have been lawful in Ireland (such as where the mother's life would not have been at risk), then the Irish courts will be prepared, in order to vindicate the provisions of Article 40.3.3, to grant an injunction to restrain the mother leaving the jurisdiction. It is true that, as Egan J. himself remarked, due to lack of proof, such cases might indeed be rare due.

Nevertheless, it seems that the prospect of injunctions in future cases is still a real possibility (if not, indeed, a probability) and that, *subject only to the right to travel to avail of services under Community law,* such injunctions will be granted in future cases where the Irish courts deem this necessary or appropriate. This decision will probably prove to be an uncomfortable one for the present Government, which is opposed, in principle, to the very possibility of travel restrictions being imposed.

What is inevitable is that this decision may prove to have considerable significance for the Maastricht referendum and the problem arises in this way. We have just seen that Article 40.3.3 may still be successfully invoked to prevent such a woman leaving the jurisdiction. While this seems to be a consequence of Article 40.3.3, nonetheless, this constitutional provision may have to yield to the supremacy of Community law and, in particular, the right under the present *state of Community law* to travel abroad to avail of services in other member states. It is at this point that the Protocol may assume significance. If it is only Community law which ensures the right to travel abroad in all cases (and irrespective of whether, for example, the right to life of the mother is at issue), then the effect of the Protocol may be to deprive litigants of their right to rely on *Community law rights in abortion cases arising in Ireland.*

In other words, the plain words of the Protocol appear to state that, henceforth, once it is ratified, Community law cannot be impleaded in abortion cases arising in Ireland to qualify or negative the effects of Article 40.3.3 of the Constitution of Ireland. This interpretation is disputed by some – in particular by Professors Binchy and Curtin (see *The Irish Times,* 25 February 1992 and 2 March 1992) but it is generally agreed by all sides that (a) the Protocol will supersede all other Community law within its proper area of application; (b) that the ECJ will be the ultimate arbiter of the meaning of the Protocol and (c) that the Protocol itself, being an exception to the general principles of Community law, will have to be strictly construed. Let us examine, therefore, how the Protocol may operate in practice.

If we return to the facts of the Open-Door Counselling case, we see that the provision of abortion counselling is prohibited by Article 40.3.3. Let us assume, however, that the clinics in Dublin have an "economic connection" (to use the words of the ECJ in the Grogan case) with similar clinics in England. In the ordinary way – *were it not for the Protocol –* it would seem that Dublin clinics would have the right to disseminate such information by virtue of the services provisions of Articles 59 and 60 of the Treaty of Rome. If a woman has the right under Community law to travel to another Community State to obtain an abortion, it would seem to follow that she has a co-relative right to obtain information *in this State* about the exercise of that Community right.

It is true that the exercise of these rights are (quite independently of the Protocol) at all times subject to Irish public policy, which may (or may not) possibly prevail over the exercise of these Community rights. This is something on which the ECJ has yet to rule, but to judge from the advisory opinion of Advocate-General Van Gerven, while a ban on the distribution of abortion information would be acceptable and legitimate, a domestic ban on intra-Community travel for this purpose would be invalid under Community law as a disproportionate reliance on Irish public policy.

At all events, it seems that, under the *present state of Community law* (i.e., *without the Protocol*), any ban imposed by the Irish courts on the distribution of abortion information (which itself may have to be re-examined as a matter of ordinary Irish *constitutional law* in the light of the X case) would probably be acceptable under Community law as a legitimate and proportionate invocation of Irish public policy so as to restrict the provisions of services. However, it would appear to be otherwise in the case of any travel ban, since this would seem to be a disproportionate reliance on domestic public policy and, hence, invalid under Community law.

We now come to the kernel of the dispute concerning the interpretation of the Protocol and its interaction with Irish constitutional law. As we have seen in the light of the judgment of the Supreme Court, it seems that the Irish courts may nonetheless, as a means of vindicating and enforcing Article 40.3.3, grant an injunction in abortion cases to restrain travel abroad *where the life of the mother is not an issue.* Under the present state of Community law, such an injunction would appear to be invalid. But will this still be the case if the Protocol is ratified? The answer would appear to depend on the meaning of the phrase "the application in Ireland of Article 40.3.3 of the Constitution of Ireland". To test our understanding of this phrase, let us take three different fact situations.

In our first example, let us assume that an Irish woman has travelled from Dublin to Amsterdam for the purpose of securing an abortion there. After she has arrived in the Netherlands, the Irish High Court purports to grant an injunction directing that woman not to have an abortion. Even if such an injunction could be granted as a matter of Irish law, it is probably invalid under present Community law in that it interferes with the lawful provision of services under Community law. This answer would not be affected by the ratification of the Protocol, since in this example, the injunction does not stem from the *application in Ireland of Article 40.3.3.* The injunction may have been granted to enforce Article 40.3.3, but the application of that order was not *in Ireland;* rather, it was *in the Netherlands.*

In our second example, let us assume that women's clinics in Dublin reach a commercial agreement with clinics in London whereby the former have agreed to advertise *in Dublin* the existence of abortion services in London. The Irish High Court, following the decision of the Supreme Court in the Open Door Counselling case, grants an injunction to restrain the distribution of such abortion information (assuming that Open Door Counselling has not itself been implicitly overruled by the decision in X).

Given the advisory opinion of the Advocate-General in the Grogan case, this injunction is *probably* valid, since the public policy proviso to Articles 59 and 60 of the Treaty of Rome would seem to allow Ireland to impose a ban of this kind. But if we assume that it is not valid under *existing Community law,* the Protocol will nonetheless preserve and protect the ban from future challenges under Community law, since the distribution of information in that example was "in Ireland" within the meaning of the Protocol, even *if the subject-matter of the information* related to matters outside Ireland. The information ban would thus be immune from challenge on Community law grounds, since it is a consequence of "the application in Ireland of Article 40.3.3".

Finally, for our third example, let us assume that the case of an adult Irish woman who is pregnant, but who is not suicidal and who wishes to have an abortion in England, comes before the Irish courts. The Irish High Court, in order to vindicate and enforce Article 40.3.3, grants an injunction restraining that woman from leaving the country. Can that woman rely on Community law to ensure that she has the right to leave the State? In view of the provisions of the Protocol, it would seem not, since an injunction would not be extra-territorial in either its operation or effect (since it is directed to an Irish woman within Ireland).

In truth, such an injunction would be a direct consequence of the application "in Ireland of Article 40.3.3 of the Constitution of Ireland", just as much as the imposition of the information ban represented the "application in Ireland" of Article 40.3.3. The fact that in both cases, the person concerned wishes either to travel to Britain to have an abortion or to receive information within Ireland about abortion facilities in Britain does not give either case a trans-national dimension, assuming the persons concerned are within the jurisdiction of the Irish courts and have not left the country.

The foregoing analysis has proved to be controversial with some commentators. For example, Professor Curtin wrote in *The Irish Times* on March 2, 1992:

The (ECJ) will not allow the precise and limited scope of the wording used in the Protocol to be interpreted in a manner that would result in a significant derogation for Ireland from existing well-established and fundamental tenets of Community law such as the supremacy of Community law over all national law. It follows that the (ECJ) will not allow the protocol to be used by the Irish state to protect injunctions preventing pregnant women from travelling abroad from Community law scrutiny.

It may be said, however, that this ovelooks the fact that the Protocol *will itself become part of Community law* upon ratification. It is not so much a case of the Irish courts attempting to give precedence to domestic constitutional law in preference to Community law, rather that the Protocol itself states that, as *a matter of Community law,* nothing in the Treaty of Rome or the Treaty of European Union can affect the proper application within Ireland of Article 40.3.3. This is no different from any other form of derogation (which is already a common place within Community law) or, indeed, the various other Protocols annexed to the Maastricht Treaty, ranging from the special protection given to Danish legislation on the acquisition of second homes to the special provision given to the United Kingdom with regard to the Social Charter.

In the immediate aftermath of the Supreme Court judgements in the X case, the Government sought first to have the Maastricht Protocol amended so as to secure rights to travel and information to Irish citizens wishing to travel abroad to obtain an abortion. It was originally thought that the other eleven member states would readily agree to an amendment to the Protocol in advance of the ratification process. This proved more difficult than had originally been anticipated and, ultimately, it transpired to be impossible.

Other countries were unwilling to re-open the issue, fearing that it might lead to a wholescale revision of the Maastricht Treaty. The Government then promised that it would sponsor a new constitutional referendum to secure the right to travel and to information, but it concluded that this was not feasible in advance of the Maastricht referendum itself. This left the difficulty that the Protocol would arguably still have the effect of removing Community law rights to travel and information in abortion cases arising "in Ireland" (a consequence regarded unacceptable by the Government), while those wishing to secure these rights would have to wait for another referendum on these issues.

Although the other member states were unwilling to amend the Protocol, they were willing to issue a Solemn Declaration in the following terms:

The High Contracting Parties to the Treaty on European Union signed at Maastricht on the 7th day of February 1992.

Having considered the terms of Protocol No. 17 to the said Treaty on European Union which is annexed to the Treaty and to the Treaties establishing the European Communities;

Hereby give the following legal interpretation: that it was and is their intention that the Protocol shall not limit freedom either to travel between Member States or, in accordance with conditions which may be laid down, in conformity with Community law, by Irish legislation, information relating to services lawfully available in Member States.

At the same time, the High Contracting Parties solemnly declare that, in the event of a future constitutional amendment in Ireland which concerns the subject matter of Article 40.3.3 of the Constitution of Ireland and which does not conflict with the intention of the High Contracting Parties hereinbefore expressed, they will, following the entry into force of the Treaty on European Union, be favourably disposed to amending the said Protocol so as to extend its application to such constitutional amendment if Ireland so requests.

As a statement of *future* political intent and understanding, the Declaration itself is unexceptionable. But – as we shall presently see – what is difficult to accept is the assertion that the member states at all times had interpreted the Protocol to mean that it should not affect the right to travel and information.

While the promise to consider amending the Protocol, should this prove to be necessary in the wake of further constitutional changes in Ireland, doubtlessly has value as a political promise, that part of the Declaration which purports to give a legal interpretation to the Protocol and to state that it was not intended to affect travel or information rights would not appear to have any legal standing whatever. It is true that the European Court is more willing than our courts to look to preparatory working documents (such as reports prepared by specialists prior to the drafting of legislation) in order to assist it in the interpretation of the ultimate texts, but even then it does not do so often and, in any event, the preparatory texts are only used as a guide and cannot bind the European Court of Justice.

More importantly, this principle is by definition, confined to *preparatory texts*. Moreover, it appears that there were no such preparatory documents laid before the Inter Governmental Conference prior to the negotiation of the Protocol. We know this because when the Supreme Court asked for such documents during the argument in the X case, they were told by counsel for the State that there were none. This fact alone underlines the essentially hollow nature of the Solemn Declaration, as a form of legal assurance, and this is also re-enforced by the assertion by the High Contracting Parties in the Declaration that they had always interpreted the Protocol to mean that it should not affect the rights to travel or to information.

Concerning what we may term as the retrospective claim made in the Solemn Declaration, we have already seen that the Protocol appears to have been a response to the decision of the European Court in the Grogan case and the vulnerability of the absolute information ban to a Community law-based-challenge in a future case. In other words, insofar as one can glean, the intentions of the drafters of the Protocol, they seem to have envisaged – contrary to the assertions contained in the Solemn Declaration – protecting the then-existing ban on the provision of information in abortion cases imposed by the Supreme Court. Secondly, if in December 1991 the Government did have an understanding with its Community partners that the Protocol (and, by implication, Article 40.3.3) did not have the effect of restricting travel, then the question arises: why did the Attorney General commence an action in February 1992 seeking to restrict an Irish citizen leaving the State where she sought to have an abortion in Britain? The answer must be that at the time there had been no such understanding, or the Attorney-General surely would not have acted in a manner inconsistent with that understanding.

One further issue must also be considered. At the present time of writing (April 1992), the possibility is still open that the Government will sponsor yet a further amendment which would have the effect of reversing the decision in the X case insofar as that judgement permitted limited abortion in this State. This raises the question: is the Article 40.3.3 referred to in the Protocol that which existed at the time of ratification of the Maastricht Treaty or would it embrace any future constitutional amendment of that provision?

This question is a novel one, raising fundamental questions concerning the precise inter-relationship of Community and domestic law. On the one hand, legal certainty would seem to require that our

Community partners should only be bound by that version of Article 40.3.3 as existed at the time of the ratification of the Treaty. On the other hand, it may plausibly be argued that the intention of the Protocol was to commit these matters entirely to the provenance of Irish constitutional law. If this argument is correct, it would mean that the Protocol includes any future changes to Article 40.3.3, at least where those changes were in harmony with the spirit of the original version of that provision. There is much force in both arguments, but if the former argument is correct, it gives rise to the difficulty that ratification of the Treaty and Protocol might have the effect of 'freezing' Article 40.3.3 as it presently stands (i.e., in the sense that if Article 40.3.3 were changed by referendum, it might not enjoy the protection of the Protocol in that it only refers to the 'original' Article 40.3.3). Of course, it is in this connection that the Solemn Declaration may prove valuable, in that it effectively represents a promise to convene an Inter Governmental Conference after the ratification of the Maastricht Treaty with a view to amending the Protocol should this prove necessary.

Conclusion

It is undoubtedly ironic that a special Protocol designed to ensure that the abortion question did not come to dominate the Maastricht referendum debate has itself ensured that the abortion question will not be far from the surface if the Protocol remains in place in its present form. Reviewing the situation at the time of writing:

(a) The Irish courts can still grant injunctions in an appropriate case to restrain travel where the woman concerned intends to have an abortion which would be unlawful in Ireland (though undertakings have been given on behalf of the Attorney General that no such injunctions would be sought after 18th June should the referendum be approved);

(b) such a ban would probably be unlawful under the present state of *Community law;*

(c) the Maastricht Protocol (No. 17) will ensure that, in any future case, the woman concerned will not be entitled to rely on Community law to assert her right to travel, provided she is still within the jurisdiction of the Irish courts when the injunction is granted, as this is the application 'in Ireland' of Article 40.3.3;

(d) that the Solemn Declaration, while containing a useful promise of political intent and a commitment to further action should this prove necessary, does not of itself constitute a binding legal interpretation of the Protocol.

It would seem, therefore, that if the Government wishes to ensure that injunctions of the kind already granted by the High Court in the X case are not granted in some future case, then it will be necessary, at a minimum, to amend the Protocol (which step, of course, has already been ruled out in advance of ratification) to ensure that it does not prejudice the *Community law* right to travel. Even this may not be enough to meet the Government's objectives, since we cannot be certain (especially in the light of the judgement of Costello J.) that the Community law right to travel will take precedence over Article 40.3.3, bearing the *existing Community law public policy exception in mind*. Perhaps the only way in which this objective will be securely achieved would be to sponsor (as the government has promised to do) a constitutional amendment expressly guaranteeing the right to travel and ensuring that this took precedence *as a matter of Irish constitutional law* over the provisions of Article 40.3.3.

IRELAND AND THE UNION

15. ISSUES

Brendan Halligan

Chapter 13 has outlined the reasons why a referendum on the Maastricht Treaty is constitutionally necessary. Strictly speaking, a referendum is an instrument to amend the wording of the constitution but in political terms a referendum on Europe is more akin to a plebiscite in which the people are asked for their verdict on an important issue of national policy. The two previous referendums of 1972 and 1987 worked out that way in practice and doubtlessly this debate will be of a similar nature.

In 1972, the case for joining the European Economic Community (EEC), as it was then called, was presented almost exclusively in economic terms with heavy emphasis on the benefits to be derived from membership. The political aims which had led to the creation of the EEC in the first place were never seriously debated. A Government White Paper on Ireland's proposed entry had pointedly referred to the fact that the economic integration of Europe on the basis of the EEC was no more than a means to a political end. Regrettably, this was forgotten. The understandable enthusiasms for guaranteed agricultural prices and access to wider industrial markets meant that political considerations were largely ignored. They received little public attention in the following decade and a half.

The 1987 referendum on the Single European Act was held after a General Election which had exhausted both the parties and the public. The debate was relatively low key and the turnout disturbingly low. Once again the arguments in favour of ratification depended heavily on economic advantages, focusing on the enhanced Structural Funds and the creation of the Single Market. The renewed impetus towards closer union among the member states of what was now known as the European Community (EC) excited little political comment, except for exaggerated fears that neutrality would be endangered by the process of European Political Cooperation as codified within the Act.

Looking back, both referendums stand out for their preoccupation with the economic consequences of Ireland's involvement in Europe rather than with the nature of the political commitment demanded from those countries seeking to join the EEC and then deciding to remain within it. Looking at the present, it can be said the Irish electorate have yet to debate and pronounce upon European unity as an ambition for altering the relations between the countries of Europe. There remains a disturbing lack of knowledge as to why the project of European unification was undertaken some forty years ago and of the process by which it is to be achieved. Looking to the immediate future, it is clear that the Maastricht Treaty makes such a debate and decision essential. On this occasion the debate will have to go far beyond purely economic considerations or a conglomeration of single issues; the decision will have to be political in the broadest sense of the word.

A New Phase

The main justification for this contention is that Maastricht marks a new phase in the process of creating an ever closer union amongst the peoples of Europe, to quote its own words. The economic basis of that intended 'closer union' has been well and truly laid by the Rome Treaties, the Single European Act and the common policies erected upon them. The intention now is to construct a political union alongside its economic counterpart, which has, after all, been four decades in the making. It is precisely for this reason that the Treaty creates a new entity called the 'European Union' which is to be a marriage of the economic and the political and with the potential for evolving into some form of federation. Inevitably, this implies the member states will in future increasingly share important elements of political as well as economic sovereignty in common, thereby altering the relations between them and, collectively, with the rest of the world.

The Treaty of Maastricht is not a blueprint for a federation of European States and it may not even represent the threshold of that ambition, but it is an unmistakable step in that direction. Arguably, it is the first real step. The central question in the referendum should logically be whether or not the Irish people wish to be part of an enterprise which might in time lead to political as well as economic unity among the peoples of Europe.

That is a political choice. It goes to the heart of our vision of ourselves as a people and of the role we wish to play in the world. It necessarily involves a judgement as to how we wish to exercise our national sovereignty and best advance our own interests, both political and economic. Viewed in these terms, the decision to be made can be reduced to a choice between two options; is Ireland to commit itself to the European Union about to be created and remain within the process of integration or is it to opt out and choose some form of external relationship? That question was not answered politically in 1972 or 1987. The Treaty of Maastricht puts it back on the table for debate and decision. On this occasion, it should be unambiguously resolved, one way or the other.

European Union

Why should Ireland commit itself to the goal of European Union and remain within a process which progressively limits its national sovereignty? What benefits, both political and economic, are likely to arise and are they greater than the costs which will inevitably be incurred? Is a return to a more traditional form of independence likely to serve our national interests better?

These questions legitimately belong to the referendum debate and demand credible answers before the electorate adjudicates on Maastricht. The previous chapters have attempted to provide a coherent analysis of the issues involved by placing them in their proper historical and political context. The purpose of this particular chapter is to draw them together in what is intended as a logical framework in which the issues facing the electorate can be evaluated.

The starting point is the political objective of European unification, which set the process of integration in train some forty years ago and which still drives it forward. The aim of replacing successive wars based on historic divisions in Europe by a voluntary unity based on political and economic interdependence is obviously no small goal. The reversal of hundreds of years of mutual antagonism, racial hatred and recurrent war (which had led France and Germany to fight each other three times in seventy years) is as big an undertaking as one could conceive. Yet those who embarked upon it after the end of World War II believed that

Europe had no other future. An entirely new structure based on political and economic interdependence was needed to replace poisonous divisions rooted in narrow nationalism. It was this conviction which inspired some political leaders to commence the task of reconstructing Europe on lines which up to then had appeared impossible.

History may still prove that ambition to be unrealisable but the process is now well advanced and the Treaty of Maastricht is intended to extend it even further through a series of measures which would, among other things, provide a collective political leadership based on the Heads of Government meeting in the European Council, lay the foundations of a single economy through economic and monetary union, inaugurate a common foreign and security policy, initiate cooperation in home and judicial affairs, extend the policy range of the existing Community, expand financial assistance to underdeveloped regions such as Ireland, confer common citizenship on the nationals of the member states and create a framework for the greater democratic control of common institutions.

Taken together (along with the many other initiatives analysed in the earlier chapters) these measures indicate beyond question that what is at issue here is more than a change of name from a European Community to a European Union. The change is in the character of the integration process itself and Maastricht could be said to mark the end of the first phase, stretching back over forty years, and the commencement of the second. From now on the focus is to be both political and economic whereas previously it was predominantly economic. If Maastricht is ratified and its provisions implemented as planned, then the goal of European unification will have been moved from the realm of the possible to that of the probable. That is what is at stake in this referendum.

A Question Of Identity

It may be argued in reply that this is naive idealism rather than political realism and that in the world of realpolitik the vision of a Europe united, peaceful and prosperous, is no more than a pipe dream. This is possibly true. But so far, the founding idealism has been accompanied by a hard headed pragmatism based on the Monnet method which concentrates on concrete achievements as the building blocks of the new Europe. The integration process has generated political momentum on the basis mainly of economic success and the result is a degree of inter-dependence which would have seemed inconceivable in the Europe prior to the outbreak of the war. So too would a half century of peace between West European states.

It is proper, in the world of politics, to temper idealism with the antidote of scepticism. The goal of a united Europe, at peace with itself and the outside world, may indeed be proven impossible by history. But in moral terms the prize is so great that it has to be attempted. Leaving aside for the moment the economic benefits which integration has so far brought us, the question to be answered at some point is whether the Irish people believe this political ambition is one in which they should share. Maastricht offers a golden opportunity because it marks a turning point in which the political aspect of integration begins to take on real substance. If, on the other hand, the debate follows a similar pattern to those of 1972 and 1987, then the real meaning of the Treaty will have been overlooked in terms of its grand design. Instead, it will be evaluated either on economic calculations or else on public reaction to single issues. We will once again have missed seeing the wood for the trees.

The two previous referendums mistook the process for the purpose, confused the means of integration with the end objective, concentrated on the economic to the detriment of the political. There are many reasons why the wood should have been overlooked in favour of the trees; our relative isolation from the wider Europe (particularly in terms of language), our singular historic experience as a people and what can only be described as our collective good fortune in escaping the trauma of a world war. But understandable as they may be for our past psychological indifference towards European unity, they cannot suffice on this occasion either as an excuse or explanation for avoiding the main question posed by Maastricht; do we wish to be part of the process towards a united Europe or do we prefer for whatever reason to limit, and possibly end, our involvement now?

Ultimately, the answer must be a political one, for economic self interest can only carry us so far. It is more a matter of psychological disposition as anything else. Indeed, what is basically at issue in this referendum is the age old question of political identity and allegiance. In the opening decades of this century we determined by democratic choice that we were Irish not British. As the century draws to a close a new question arises. Are we not just Irish, but European as well? All other issues are subsidiary.

An Ever Widening Process

Chapter 11 on the enlargement of the Union has indicated that other European states have had to face the same question at different times. Originally, the Coal and Steel Community and its successor, the European Economic Community, had but six members. It is well to recall that membership was then open to any democratic state in Europe but that some, including Ireland, declined to join. The economic success of the EEC led to Great Britain revising its opposition and gaining admission in 1973, with Denmark and Ireland deciding to do likewise in the belief their trading relationships with Britain and the then EEC left them with no viable alternative. Three other states, Greece, Spain and Portugal, were later to opt for membership on the political grounds that being inside the EEC would secure their recently-restored democracies from internal threat. In essence, the first four decades of integration have been characterised by the successive geographic widening of the process.

Now the European Community, or more properly the European Union, is likely to be expanded yet again. Three neutral states have applications on the table (Austria, Sweden and Finland) and may well be joined by the remaining three EFTA states (Norway, Switzerland and Iceland). Furthermore, the three Central European states of Poland, Czechoslovakia and Hungary are jointly intent on membership by the end of the century. In addition, there are other European countries which have already applied for membership or indicated their intention of doing so.

These political realities bear repeating in order to identify what should be the second main issue in the debate. The process of integration not only involves the deepening of the relationship between the participating member states but also of widening the numbers involved. By the end of this century the process will have been underway for about fifty years and the number of member states will have gone from six to around twenty. In geographic terms the European Union will then extend from the Atlantic to the borders of the CIS, and from the Arctic Ocean to the Mediterranean Sea. In other words, it will encompass the greater part of what we commonly call 'Europe'.

This is not to argue that all the member states of such an enlarged union will share equally in the goal of uniting Europe in something approximating to a federation. It is self evident that those which joined after the Treaty of Rome were driven mainly by pragmatic considerations; the first group by what it regarded as good economic reasons and the

129

second by political self interest. The next phase of enlargement seems set to repeat that pattern. But whatever the motivation for joining, the main point for emphasis is that by the century's end the European Union will in all probability include most democratic states which call themselves European.

If these circumstances came to pass, where would we wish to be as a people? Do we want to be part of a family of countries committed, at the very least, to a greater degree of interdependence than attains at present in the European Community or do we prefer to exclude ourselves from that process? Effectively speaking, the choice is between involvement in, or isolation from, this new Europe.

Economic Sovereignty

The answer to the question of involvement or isolation depends on our vision of ourselves as a people, and is essentially one of political identity. It cannot be treated solely in economic terms, important as they may be. The Maastricht Treaty puts the issue of national independence right at the centre of the referendum debate because that European Union would require us to share elements of political as well as economic sovereignty with its other member states. Unavoidably, this raises the question of what we believe the essence of sovereignty to be and the extent to which we are prepared to have it circumscribed through joint action with other countries.

The electorate has already given part of the answer by ratifying entry into the EEC in 1972 and by endorsing the Single European Act in 1987. Both those Treaties imposed limits on the exercise of sovereignty in the economic sphere, notably in terms of trade policy. The decision to join the EMS in 1979 introduced further limitations, in this instance relating to exchange rate policy. So far none of these encroachments have been judged as infringing on Irish independence to an unacceptable extent. Indeed, the contrary observation can be made. By pooling economic sovereignty within the EC, the Irish state has been better able to protect its interests than would have been the case outside. The validity of that judgement can be gauged from our national experience during the first fifty years of statehood when, for example, the agricultural sector suffered from a low price regime externally imposed, and monetary policy, including the exchange rate, was determined to all intents and purposes by another country.

130

Given the benefits of the CAP, the Structural Funds and other financial transfers from the EC, it can be concluded that the Irish electorate judge the advantages flowing from shared economic sovereignty to be greater than the loss of either formal or nominal independence. With the advent of strengthened policies on Cohesion (such as those outlined in Chapter 7) and the free trade obligations arising from future GATT agreements, it is highly unlikely that this judgement will be changed in the future. In a small open economy dependent on international trade to a unique degree, this conviction is likely to strengthen rather than weaken with the passage of time.

The same is true even for economies as large as the German or French. As the Albert and Ball Report (commissioned for the European Parliament in 1982/83) demonstrated, no national economy in Europe can be independently managed and a high degree of coordination is required collectively if those economies are to prosper individually. The days of economic nationalism are not only numbered but long gone.

Is the same true of sovereignty in the political sphere?

Political Sovereignty

To an extent this is an artificial question, for sovereignty cannot be split in practice into two self-contained entities, the economic and the political, which can be kept separate from each other. A society which fails economically will have little real capacity to assert its political independence and conversely economic success enhances the scope for independent political action. Furthermore, certain elements of economic sovereignty, such as the exchange rate in the UK or the role of the Bundesbank in the German Federal Republic, are often taken as important symbols of nationhood. In policy terms, the management of the economy is as much a matter of politics as it is of economics.

Despite these qualifications, political sovereignty lies at the centre of the referendum debate, and indeed in simultaneous debates in many other member states. If not resolved unambiguously by us, then our participation in the integration process could be put at risk, irrespective of the economic advantages to be gained from membership. As a nation which struggled so long for independence we do not need to be reminded that at heart the question is the right of a people to a system of government in accordance with their own wishes. Basically, this is a psychological phenomenon concerning the consent of the governed to be governed.

Within Europe particularly, nations with their own sense of separate identify demand that authority should be embodied in their own state and where this is denied conflict inevitably erupts, as contemporary events so tragically confirm.

How then can the role of the nation state be reconciled with the goal of European Unity? Is there not a tension between the two phenomena? The direct answer is that there is, and always will be. If economic nationalism is effectively dead the same is not true of its political counterpart for the reason that national identities will always. endure. But states enter into treaties when it is in their self interest to do so and volunteer to accept the consequential limitations on their sovereignty, notably in the security sphere. The tension between independence and interdependence is reconciled on the basis of perceived mutual advantage. More importantly, from a psychological view point, such treaties are regarded as an expression of sovereign will in the interest of the common good and thereby find their validation within the democratic system.

The European Union, is a sophisticated framework in which the competing demands of separateness and mutual dependence can be accommodated. The balance between the two as proposed in the Treaty has been accepted by the more powerful national states, like Germany and France, and equally by the smaller, such as the Benelux countries. The applicant nation states must be judged as finding that balance compatible with their own views on political sovereignty.

Some of the recently emerged nation states of the former USSR and Yugoslavia take the view that membership of the Union would not only be an expression of their newly acquired independence but a guarantee of it. Certain regions argue that the separate nationhood to which they aspire can best be achieved in the context of a united Europe. There is a common view here that in a world of political interdependence and global markets, sovereignty can be best expressed by being involved in the councils of a continental sized organisation. Being at the top table is preferable to remaining outside the council room, as has been remarked by the prime minister of one applicant state.

These observations confirm that the European Union corresponds simultaneously with the psychological desire for political sovereignty and the need for greater interdependence precisely because it is based on the assent of the nation states comprising it. One of the Treaty's common provisions which establishes the new Union expressly acknowledges the national identities of the member states, whose systems of Goverrment are founded on the principles of democracy. If anything can be regarded as the bed rock of European unity then this is it; nation states, democracy, the rule of law, agreement to act together only on the basis of consent and such common action as is needed to ensure mutual benefit. It is on these principles that national sovereignty and European unity is being reconciled.

The question yet to be answered is whether this framework conforms with our own national aspirations. There are numerous indications to date that it may not.

Superstate

The fear of a European Superstate has been advanced against the ratification of Maastricht, both in relation to the autonomy of our national constitution and system of laws and to our right to pursue an independent common foreign and security policy based on the principles of neutrality. In both cases the European Union is conceived as a highly centralised political system with an autocratic centre dictating to what would effectively be no more than regions. This imagery finds a ready response within the Irish psyche, for good reason. Put in these terms the goal of European unity can be presented as being wholly negative in which we are asked (or forced) to "give up" our national independence.

The first of these criticisms is unfounded. It demonstrates either lack of knowledge of the origins, aim and processes of integration or a misrepresentation of them which borders on caricature. This is not to doubt that in many instances the fears of a superstate are sincerely held but is rather to assert that they are seriously mistaken because the analysis running through previous chapters, in particular those in Parts One and Two, indicates that political integration is a process in which authority flows upwards from the member states to the common institutions of the Union, and not the other way round as the protagonists of the superstate allege.

The principle of subsidiarity, the guiding constitutional principle in the Treaty, means that decisions in a political system are to be taken at the lowest effective level and in the context of European unity this requires the maximum amount of autonomy to be retained at national level and the minimum at the level of the Union. In other words, the system of government will be one in which power continues to be widely diffused in accordance with the requirements of democracy. That which resides at the higher level of the Union will be no more and no less than what is voluntarily conceded by the member states in order to achieve their common objectives.

This system of shared sovereignty has been in operation for four decades. Nothing in that experience could corroborate the charge that any member state has been coerced against its will into amending its constitution or laws. The present proposal to deepen integration is based on the integrity of the member states and on the principle of subsidiarity. Taken together they ensure that there is nothing in the Treaty which could be taken as a pointer towards some external authority empowered to impose constitutional change on the member states. Neither is there anything inherent in the dynamics of integration which would justify the fear that they will be progressively drained of any right to determine their own constitutions and systems of law.

Probably the reason why the Maastricht framework for balancing sovereignty and interdependence still gives rise to misgivings, despite the evidence of the past and the present, is our inherent distrust of any power centre outside the island. If that be so, then any commitment to European unity requires a change in the national psyche. Otherwise, there will always be fears that, for example, abortion or divorce could be externally inserted into our laws. The assertion of reputable commentators and authorities to the contrary will not be believed. Mechanisms for Ireland being involved in economic integration while detached from the political will constantly be sought as panaceas. If none are available, and if the fears persist, then the conclusion is self evident. Some form of external association would be the only way forward for those who think in this vein.

Such a policy would be based on a false premise since a European Superstate is not on the cards and would fly in the face of common sense. Few parts of the world contain such a diversity of cultural, religious, ethnic or regional differences as Europe. To suggest that some homogeneous value system could be imposed on over four hundred million people in twenty or more states is to disregard the strength of that diversity, which is one of the most enduring and endearing features of the continent. The fact that it can be suggested and debated seriously is salutary proof that the forces against European unity owe more to the legacy of history than to an understanding of contemporary politics. Perhaps one of the problems is the political vocabulary used in discussions about the goal of eventual unity.

The term 'union' can be taken to imply uniformity, and federation to point towards a strong central executive. In these interpretations of what was originally conceived as the future for Europe and what is still intended, the process of integration can be taken as one of centralisation and therefore something to be feared as a latter day version of *pax romana*. If that were the case, the process should not only be feared but resisted. But it is not the case. Monnet and other founders of the Community sought the unity of peoples through a structured inter-dependence of the states to which they gave their primary loyalty. It was hoped over time to create a second loyalty to the continent which these peoples and states shared in common, a loyalty which would complement rather than supplant. There is no single word which can sum up this aspiration intelligibly and, in that, the vocabulary of integration is deficient in transmitting the meaning of its objective and of the means by which it is to be achieved.

Interdependence is possibly the best term at hand to convey the sense of what is being attempted. Shared sovereignty is probably the best description of what is actually being done by the member states within the institutions of the Community. Until such time as a better vocabulary emerges the aim of unification under the title of 'Union' will have to suffice. But, meantime, it neither warrants the label of a superstate nor justifies the allegation of centralism by stealth. Interdependence is a novel experiment in political organisation, one which is based on the sovereignty of nation states and simultaneously on their need to cooperate together. It is the concept of Community written on a larger canvas than that to which we are accustomed. In that sense, it should be welcomed rather than feared.

Neutrality

The prospect of pooling political sovereignty with other countries within a European Union has properly raised the question of our right to pursue a foreign and security policy based on the values of neutrality. For many, neutrality is the most potent symbol of our national independence and will be an issue of concern even for those who would have little difficulty in accepting the logic of economic integration and many areas of the political. Therefore the question demands the most rigorous examination, not least to deal further with the fear of a superstate, which in this instance is presented in a military guise.

The origins of Irish neutrality go back beyond the foundations of the state and first found concrete expression in the national decision not to become embroiled in the World War II. Viewed in the context of a colonised people who had won their freedom less than two decades previously this was a clear manifestation of independence from the former colonial power. Neutrality later took on a wider political content, largely within the context of our membership of the United Nations and the relations developed with Third World countries, most of which had shared the same history of colonisation. Neutrality, as a policy, became to be based on a system of values having at their heart an antipathy to militarism and an aversion to power blocs, which were frequently seen as another form of exploitation. From a moral standpoint, their values are an important expression of the principles on which international relations should be based and are a necessary corrective to what remains of the imperialist tendency in Europe.

Most of the current members of the European Community have an imperialist past which continued long into this century. It is also true that most of those countries were engaged in World War II and subsequently regarded themselves as under the threat of Soviet expansion. These three sets of experiences are markedly different from ours and it is not surprising that our view and theirs should differ on the question of dealing with an external security threat. All belong to NATO in one form or another. We do not.

The other eleven member states have regarded a military alliance as essential to their collective security, not least those states, such as Belgium and Holland, which found their neutrality violated in previous world wars. For them, political independence and membership of an alliance are complementary. Indeed, the alliance is the precondition of their independence, whereas for us, remaining outside all military alliances is an expression of independence. It is natural for them to regard the collective security of the European Union as eventually requiring a common defence policy, which might in time evolve into its common defence. Chapter 9 on the Common Foreign and Security Policy pillar of the proposed Union makes it clear that common defence, or even a common policy on defence, is not part of the Treaty. Nevertheless, there is a commitment within it to consider an eventual common defence policy by 1996 and for the foreign ministers to submit a report on the matter to the European Council, consisting of the Heads of

Government,who may or may not decide to act on it. If they decide not to, then Ireland's neutrality will not be at issue.

New Security Situation

If there is a desire to go to the next stage of political union, thereby involving some move towards a common defence policy, can Ireland subscribe to this development? Perhaps the most illuminating way of answering that question is by reference to the three neutral states intent on joining the Union after Maastricht is ratified. Their applications for membership have been tabled in the full knowledge that a common defence policy is to be examined and put before the European Council shortly after their arrival as full members. This indicates they see no incompatability between their existing policy stances and membership of the European Union. The same applies to Switzerland which has recently signalled its intention of joining at some future stage. The proximate cause for this judgement on their part is doubtlessly the break up of the Soviet empire and the disappearance of the Warsaw Pact.

NATO itself is currently re-evaluating its role in the new circumstances obtaining in Europe and is actually faced with the prospect of some of its former adversaries seeking membership as a means of ensuring their own security. The formation of the North Atlantic Cooperation Council bringing NATO and the Commonwealth of Independent States together around the one table is a dramatic reminder of how much the international scene has altered in three years and how old adversarial relationships have changed. As a further example of this change, the CSCE has recently embarked upon a major conference in Helsinki which could provide the basis for pan-European security structures amongst its fifty member states.

However, old attitudes have not completely changed in some member states and there are those who still think in the categories of Cold War politics, such as favouring a continued role for the US in maintaining European security. Their influence, although not predominant, can be detected in the Treaty provisions on Common Foreign and Security Policy. Others have responded to some extent to the new realities and are moving towards a pan-European view of security which could involve the CIS.

As in all systems of decision-making there is a complex mix of continuity and change and it would be disingenuous to forecast which of these tendencies will predominate at the Inter Governmental Conference in 1996. Change may be externally generated, as Patrick Keatinge remarks in Chapter 9, and there could be a number of surprises, both nasty and pleasant, in store which would require major reorientations in security policy. Aside from these rather obvious comments about the unpredictability of the future security situation, one significant change would mark the 1996 conference.

By that time the membership of the Union should have been expanded to include three, and possibly four neutrals, and it is conceivable, but not certain, the three applicants from Central Europe will be consulted as potential members (analogous to our involvement in the 1972 Paris Summit and that of Spain and Portugal prior to the SEA in 1987). This suggests that Ireland's position at the conference table will be strengthened immeasurably since the values of neutrality will have to be taken as the policy principles of a significant minority of the actual and potential Union membership and not just as the stance of one small member. Any reasonable interpretation of this development would conclude that the character of the debate on a common defence policy will be altered and that it would be premature simply to extrapolate Cold War policies based on the 1980s to the new conditions of the late 1990s.

The 1996 Conference

Security policy in the area of common defence is demonstrably in a state of flux, but the key question will remain, against whom do the states of Western and Central Europe defend themselves and by what means? However, the identity of a potential external aggressor has become blurred, particularly when former enemies now sit at the same table in the North Atlantic Cooperation Council. Is there, in these circumstances, a need to have a centralised command system similar to NATO or should the security of Europe be based on a looser common defence pact incorporating the principle of mutual assistance in the event of attack? These questions are likely to figure as key agenda items in the forthcoming consideration of a common defence policy and the very fact that a policy still has to be agreed is conclusive proof that the answers have not yet been formulated. The revival of the long-dormant WEU, which now sits uneasily between NATO and the EC, is an attempt to give a 'European' as opposed to an 'Atlanticist' answer. Few observers are convinced that it does. Any pretence that answers were found at

Maastricht is either a misrepresentation of the provisions of the Treaty or a misunderstanding of the dynamics of integration.

For Ireland, the questions to be answered are, does a European Union at some point involve its member states in the defence of that Union and, if so, how are these obligations to be discharged. The White Paper of 1970 implied that a political union would logically require its common defence, even on the basis of solidarity. It indicated that this country should be willing to engage in whatever measures were thought necessary. This view point has been repeated by successive Taoisigh, but in truth, the issue has never been subjected to sustained public debate.

It is time that it was, not least because the provisions of the CFSP make it possible to ratify the Maastricht Treaty without prejudice to the policy of neutrality. The debate could commence and be continued up to the convening of the IGC. Any conclusions emerging by way of consensus could then be employed in developing a common position with the other neutrals within the IGC with particular reference to the objectives of preserving peace and strengthening international security in accordance with the principles of the UN Charter and the Helsinki Final Act, as well as with the objectives of the revived CSCE. These principles and objectives would undoubtedly continue as the basis of our own security policy and we would seek to give them concrete expression in any common policy presented to the Heads of Government.

If the European Council subsequently pronounces unanimously on a future Common Defence Policy, the proposals could then be judged by the Irish people in another referendum on the basis of whatever national consensus had emerged. As Chapter 13 makes clear, any departure from neutrality would necessitate a further referendum and, hence, neither the debate nor the decision on future security policy can be pre-empted by ratification of the Treaty.

This brings the argument full circle. Our vision of ourselves as a people and of our role in Europe would take on a crucial importance in the IGC. A self-confident Ireland, with a coherent policy as to how an expanded Union was to contribute to the peace of Europe and the wider world, could make a distinctive contribution to the outcome. It would be proactive in propagating the values which have to date underlain our neutrality. An inward-looking Ireland would be silent in such a forum and would doubtlessly withdraw from the challenge of thinking through new strategies for changed circumstances. Maastricht and its aftermath offers us the choice between these two alternatives and the only people who can choose the path to be followed, are ourselves alone. The issue remains open and will not be closed off by ratification of the Treaty.

The question of agreeing a common security system for Europe is an issue in which we have a vital interest but it belongs solely to the period after Maastricht. It is a challenge to which we have have to respond with imagination whether we are in the Union or not. The challenge will be to ensure that the focus of a common defence policy would be precisely what is says; the defence of those collective interests which arise directly from common action within the institutions of the Union. As a policy position for Ireland, this would be consistent with the analysis quoted earlier from the 1970 White Paper that countries which act together politically and economically have an obligation out of solidarity to ensure each other's security.

Agreement on this principle would eschew any policy of expansion, such as feared by those who believe that Europe will not just be a superstate but a military one as well. Common security based on collective solidarity could, by contrast, provide a framework for peace, particularly in Central and Eastern Europe where the potential for inter state and ethnic violence remains great. This is the security challenge which will have to be answered by the end of this decade. Ireland could, and should, participate in providing it.

The Future Union

The analysis of the referendum issues has, up to this point, been focused on the questions which directly arise from the objective of political union. It has been argued that they should be given priority in the debate as they impinge on our sense of identity and the extent to which we are willing to reconcile our aspirations as a separate people with those of a Europe which is to be united in a series of stages. It logically follows that if we were to decide on this occasion to commit ourselves unambiguously to the ambition of a united Europe, we should subsequently formulate views as to the nature of that union and the process by which it may be realised. There is more to this than just an exercise in intellectual speculation because the structure and character of the future Union will impact on virtually all areas of political and economic life. It would make good sense to develop strategies and policies as to how that inter-relationship can be optimised.

One fundamental issue remains to be resolved and was left unfinished at Maastricht, probably because its very complexity demands further analysis. The experience of four decades of integration is not yet sufficient to enable us to forecast how the future Union will actually be organised and conceivably it could take another two decades or so before clear ideas begin to emerge. The issue in question is the federal character to be adopted by a united Europe. The requirements of democracy and the growth of regionalism would suggest that the Union will be as decentralised as possible. However, the effective coordination of economic policy would demand strong institutions, as would policies designed to ensure convergence, cohesion and common minimum standards in social services.

Irish public opinion would tend to support a diffused system of political authority for the reasons discussed earlier. At the same time, our demands for meaningful policy instruments which redistribute resources to the less favoured regions would suggest the need for a cohesive political centre. In other words, an intergovernmental system along the lines with which we are mainly familiar would be preferred for one set of objectives but a more integrated structure would be favoured for the other. There is no ready answer to this dichotomy since it requires a fundamental reappraisal of the existing decision-making system in the Community with particular reference to the relationship between the Council of Ministers and the European Parliament and the role of the Commission as the guardian of the Community ideal.

Only one point can be made with certainty. The new constitutional framework will evolve on the basis of experience and the need to solve concrete political problems as they arise in the areas of efficient government and democratic accountability. The evolutionary process of going forward in discrete steps will continue but its pace and success will depend ultimately on the quality of ideas put forward by the member states in the various Inter Governmental Conferences. That, in turn, depends on their vision for Europe and their long-term strategies for its achievement. In this regard it can hardly be argued that, with a few notable exceptions, we have distinguished ourselves as a people in contributing ideas to the task of constructing the new Europe.

A positive outcome to the referendum should be understood as being the beginning and not the end of thinking about Europe. As NESC commented some years ago, the basic requirement is to have a clearly-thought-through strategy about the future of the Union and our place within it. The issue of what kind of Ireland and what kind of Europe we desire for the future is the foundation on which all others rest and it would be prudent to embark on this analysis with as much vigour and enthusiasm as we can muster.

Economic And Monetary Union

The emphasis so far on the political elements of the debate is not to suggest that the economic issues are merely of secondary importance. For a society in the process of developing its economy and beset by a range of formidable problems, such as unemployment and emigration, this could never be the case. It would furthermore be at variance with one of the central features of the Treaty if an analysis of its provisions and their implications were to be confined to the political. The framework offered in this chapter has been for the purpose of logically ordering the issues rather than prioritising them.

Aside from the new policies outlined in Chapter 5 which serve to deepen and complete the Single Market established by the Single European Act, the primary economic achievement at Maastricht was the agreement on creating an Economic and Monetary Union by 1999 at the latest. If Maastricht had done no more than this then it would still be regarded of major significance in the history of uniting Europe. The policy objectives, institutional arrangements and stages of implementation have been authoritatively examined in Chapter 6 and Rory O'Donnell has rightly commented that there is an imbalance between the monetary and economic aspects of EMU to the point where it might more properly be regarded as a monetary union.

Notwithstanding that observation, which is valid, the Treaty has achieved an objective first formally set over twenty years ago and advocated even earlier. The prospect of a single currency and a common monetary policy managed by a European Central Bank is not just of economic importance but of political significance as well. A single market with a single currency and monetary policy is well on the way to being a single economy and that, if anything, is the measure of the change introduced by Maastricht in the economic sphere.

This development has profound implications for the economic

management of all the member states. Macroeconomic policies will have to be coordinated to a greater extent than before so that, in particular, the objectives of monetary policy are met. The management of the public finances will also be affected in meeting the criteria for public debt and budget deficits laid down for entry to the final stage. In addition, the forces propelling the interpenetration of markets will be intensified and this will have consequences for competitiveness and the allocation of investment, especially internationally mobile investment on which we are so dependent.

Monetary Policy

For the Irish economy, four issues arise which are of relevance in any assessment of the impact of EMU on our economic future. The first relates to monetary policy itself. Ireland decided to enter the EMS in 1979 thereby making a commitment to a set of rules regarding the exchange rate, which effectively replaced the relationship between the Irish pound and sterling with another linking the pound to the Deutschmark. One set of limitations was replaced by another but with more beneficial results in respect of exchange rate stability, interest rates and inflation. In broad policy terms, membership of the final stage of EMU will not be any more onerous than involvement in the EMS but could well be more positive as interest rates are expected to converge and stabilise around a European norm. In summary, this aspect of EMU should not be a matter of any great controversy.

Public Debt

The situation is more problematic when it comes to evaluating the impact of the criteria for entry into the third and final stage towards the end of this decade. As Rory O'Donnell has stated, Ireland is likely to meet the requirements regarding inflation and interest rates without much difficulty. The problem arises with the limits placed on the size of the national debt. While the current borrowing level on a year-to-year basis is already below the limit set as a condition for going ahead with the move towards a single currency, the accumulation of past borrowings is substantially higher than the figure of 60 per cent of GDP as set down in the Treaty. It seems on the analysis in Chapter 6, which is widely shared, that it would be to our national advantage to join the final stage of EMU at its establishment but the size of our national debt at about 100 per cent of GDP could act as a barrier because even the best estimates suggest it

143

could only be reduced to about 80 per cent by the end of the decade. The question then to be answered is what are we to do towards overcoming this obstacle?

The point is made in Chapter 6 that the 60 per cent debt limit is likely to be interpreted as a goal towards which public debt should be moving rather than a cut off point to be rigidly applied in determining full EMU membership. This interpretation carries conviction on analysing the relevant Treaty protocol and would therefore suggest that the only way to gain entry into the final stage of EMU is to record a year on year reduction in the national debt expressed as a percentage of GDP. Clearly this is of significance for the management of the public finances as it would put limits on the growth of budgetary expenditure. This, in turn, has been criticised as a policy which would be excessively deflationary in respect of public service employment and unacceptable in terms of the quality and quantum of services to be provided by the state to the taxpayer. As such, it has been put forward as a major argument for opposing the Treaty.

At first sight this line of argumentation would seem to have credibility as an issue in the debate but the level of national debt has already been accepted by the social partners as being too high and a policy to reduce it has been successfully pursued for the past few years on the basis of a national consensus. There would appear to be no credible alternative except to continue on this path so as to restore order to the public finances with the aim of reducing an intolerably high level of debt servicing. This will have to be done as a matter of national policy, irrespective of the demands of EMU. The fact that national policy and the EMU criteria point in the same direction should be taken as a happy conjunction of policy requirements in which the two can be used to sustain each other. In these circumstances, the public debt requirements of EMU do not introduce a new and unacceptable element into public policy but rather underline the necessity of completing what we have already begun of our own volition.

Cohesion

The third issue relates to the tendency within large scale economies for the core to benefit at the expense of peripheral regions, which usually suffer not only from the diseconomies of distance but also those arising from small domestic markets. As economic integration proceeds and as the various national economies are progressively fused together the forces operating in favour of the core economy gather strength. The policy consequences of this phenomenon were not fully accepted in the Community until the mid seventies with the creation of the Regional Fund.

As Rory O'Donnell points out in Chapter 7, the case for greater assistance to the peripheral regions received a major impetus as a result of the move towards a single market in 1987. The Structural Funds were established to assist disadvantaged regions to prepare for a more competitive market in which the factors of production would be allowed to move freely across national borders. This country benefited significantly from these funds, particularly in the development of our infrastructure. In fact, Ireland receives a higher proportion of the Structural Funds than any other member state.

The move towards EMU will intensify competitive forces by transforming the Single Market to be created by the end of this year into what many commentators would describe as a single economy. The policy response of the Community is incorporated as an integral part of the Treaty and is expressed in the principle of Cohesion, which broadly means that peripheral and disadvantaged regions are to be assisted further in securing the benefits arising from a single market (or economy) and single currency.

The implementation of the principle through additional transfers, called the Cohesion Fund, is a matter for negotiation between the member states on the basis of proposals put forward by the Commission. This would follow the pattern of the Single European Act when its ratification was followed by agreement on the Structural Funds in what came to be known as the Delors package. The Commission has recently published its financial perspectives for the period 1993-1997 incorporating proposals to double the funds to the four poorest member states and negotiations are to commence later this year on its guidelines and policy consequences.

The proposals, already termed the Delors II package, will obviously be the subject of intense debate among member states since the cost of German unification is putting a severe strain on that country's capacity to fund the Community budget and the hostility of the UK to a growth in EC resources remains undiminished. Other member states have misgivings about the consequences of introducing a greater degree of progressivity into the sourcing of the Community budget. In these circumstances it would be naive to suggest that the Delors II package will go through unamended or that there is any automatic right for any member state to increased financial support. In fact, it has been argued by critics of the Treaty that the chances of Ireland doubling its receipts, via expanded Structural Funds and the new Cohesion Fund, are slight.

On a more detached level there is a formidable body of opinion which argues that a single market necessitates intra-Community transfers on a scale tantamount to what could only be described as a European federal budget. The proposed increase in the Community budget under the Delors II package of 1.2 to 1.37 per cent of aggregate GDP would fall short of what many economists believe to be necessary. Various percentages of Community GDP have been offered as the minimum threshold for a federal budget ranging from 4 to 8 per cent, and in some cases even higher. It is clear that Delors II is a long way from that.

It is possible, however, to put the proposals on increased aid to the poorer member states, which could amount in total to £6 billion for Ireland, into a context which is consistent with past experience and the actual dynamics of integration. Regional aid is now a permanent feature of Community policy and its importance is growing proportionately to the scale of integration. Each new move forward evokes a new policy response which increases the volume of aid. The move towards EMU and the Delors II package fall into this pattern and there can be no reason to doubt but that the two will go hand in hand, not least because Cohesion was written into the Maastricht Treaty as an integral part of EMU and not included as a mere adjunct. The dynamics of integration would further suggest that the scale of the Community budget will increase over time until it approaches the minimum federal threshold.

It would be unwise to confuse the normal sound and fury of Community negotiations for a retraction of the commitment to Cohesion. If EMU is to go forward then all the potential participants must have the capacity to make it operate without putting stress on the system. Putting it crudely, Structural Funds are an alternative to devaluation. The traditional remedy for a country suffering from a serious loss of competitiveness has been either devaluation or deflation (or both). EMU rules out devaluation as a policy instrument and the new Union is committed to harmonious economic development. The logic of both is that lack of competitiveness should be tackled by measures within the

146

real economy and it is this which gives Cohesion a meaning beyond the more usual connotations of equity and solidarity associated with redistribution.

What is at issue here is the capacity of a monetary union covering twelve economies to operate efficiently. Hence improvements in the infrastructure and cost base of the peripheral economies are essential if the system is to work as a totality. It is this type of rationale which justifies the conclusion that not only will the cohesion principle be implemented but that the scale of transfers will necessarily have to be significant. The size and allocation of the Structural Funds naturally remain an issue for political negotiation between the member states but the principle underlying their establishment and the reasons as to why they are necessary have already been accepted, and will not be reversed. It follows that Ireland, along with the three other member states in the same position, will benefit significantly over the medium term.

In view of the fact that Ireland, along with Spain, succeeded in having Cohesion accepted as a policy principle of political union it would make good sense to engage immediately in active negotiations on its scope and implementation, should the Treaty be ratified in the referendum.

Competitiveness

The final issue in relation to the economic aspects of Maastricht flows directly from the above analysis. Whether a European country opts to be in or out of the European Union, it will be affected by the globalisation of markets and specifically by the emergence of an integrated European economy covering over three hundred and forty million people. This will be true for any national economy irrespective of its size and will be especially true for one which is as small and open as Ireland's. Against that background it would seem that the best strategic option is to be inside the European Union as an active participant in shaping policy and as a recipient of funds which would enable us to do the things we would have to do anyway.

In that respect, the key policy requirement is to improve competitiveness on a constant basis. With exports equivalent to three quarters of our GDP, there is simply no alternative but to remain competitive, and the familiar admonition to export or die will continue to have a particularly chilling relevance for this country. It is far easier to export within an integrated market than to do so from the outside and preferable to contain costs with the assistance of external funds rather than from our own national resources. For these reasons, the range of strategic options narrows to a stark choice between membership of EMU, with the negative effects being tempered by the Structural Funds, or an external association with it in which we rely on our own resources to deal with the same set of effects.

The Economy

Membership of EMU is the most important single consequence for economic policy as a result of Maastricht. But there are many others, such as those referred to in Chapter 5, especially in relation to the operation of the Single Market. For two decades now, development policy in Ireland has been predicated on membership of the European Community, for example, our attractiveness as a location for manufacturing and services is based on access to the EC market. Our trade with member states other than the UK has expanded over the period to the point where it now exceeds that with our nearest neighbour.

This reflects our growing economic interdependence with the rest of the Community, which now accounts for three quarters of our total international trade. There is little need to stress the importance of the CAP for the agricultural sector, which will continue to play a major role in the economy. But it is necessary to emphasise what can be easily overlooked in respect of the financial market. Membership of the EC is now factored into market expectations and positively affects interest rates and equities, as well as the capacity of the Irish exchequer to raise finance abroad, particularly in Germany.

These, and many other issues which, although they cannot be individually analysed here, indicate that the Irish economy has become what the integration process is designed to achieve, a component part of a large single economy. The continuation of that relationship should be a central issue in the referendum debate for it is hard to see what alternatives exist, particularly when economies more developed than ours are set on joining the integration process. Indeed, a decision to alter or terminate our involvement in the wider European economy would constitute the greatest reversal of policy since the ending of protectionism. It is against that backdrop that the overall impact of EMU should be evaluated. Its inherent disadvantages should be balanced not just against its advantages but also against the wider consequences of reversing thirty years of policy almost overnight.

Conclusion

The issues in the referendum inevitably emerge as a combination of the political and economic but it has been suggested in the framework presented here that on this occasion the implications of political union should be analysed and debated with as much vigour as the economic. At the heart of the debate is the aim of strengthening and widening the interdependence between the European states to the point where some sort of federation emerges amongst the great majority of the democratic states in the continent. Maastricht poses a question which requires answering as to our willingness to share sovereignty with other countries and that in turn necessitates a consensus as to how we view our destiny as a people. The referendum furthermore faces us with a judgement on what is the best strategic option to be pursued in the face of economic integration leading to the creation of a single European economy. Taken together, these two fundamental issues put us at a crossroads where the choice of direction will be decisive.

16. OPTIONS

Brendan Halligan

The decision to be made in the referendum concerns Ireland's future relationship with Europe. That relationship could take on a number of different forms and consequently the range of options facing the electorate is more complex than a simple yes or no to a constitutional amendment on a ballot paper. The purpose of this chapter is to identify the more important of those options and then to analyse them in terms of their consequences for the question at issue – the place of Ireland within Europe.

The ratification or rejection of the Treaty will be assessed in terms of what either outcome *implies* as to our future intent on the process of European integration, the likely *interpretation* of the result within Ireland and the rest of the Community, the legal and political *implications* for our future relations with the European Union and, finally, its *consequences* for the Irish economy. The chapter includes a political analysis of the conundrum surrounding Protocol 17 and concludes with a broad assessment of the strategic options based on the preceding analysis.

Intent

The outcome of the referendum needs first to be examined in terms of what it would imply as the national will of the Irish people on the prospect of deepening the integration process. The importance of this examination lies in the fact that the intention of the electorate could be open to a number of different interpretations within Irish political life and, for their part, by our partners in the European Community. Any differences in interpretation could have significant implications for the manner in which our future relationship with them would evolve.

If the electorate vote in favour of the constitutional amendment, it would signify that Ireland intends to remain within the process of integration and has endorsed the establishment of the European Union. On the other hand, the rejection of the Treaty could imply a number of intentions based on quite different motivations. For example, a no vote could reflect that the Irish people wish to maintain the *status quo* within the EC by freezing the integration process at its current stage of development.

A widely canvassed version is that a no vote would represent a desire to have certain elements of the Treaty renegotiated so that a revised Treaty could be submitted to a second referendum. The intention here would be to proceed with a more diluted form of integration than that agreed at Maastricht. A negative vote could also imply that the Irish people did not wish to proceed any further with the process of unification, even if the other member states so decide. Lastly, it could be taken as an indication that Ireland intends to leave the European Community and end its involvement without further ado.

Interpretation

A positive vote would give rise to a broadly similar interpretation both within Ireland and elsewhere and would present little difficulty in terms of its policy implications for Ireland's continued relationship with the European Union. The most obvious interpretation would be that the Irish people intended to remain within the process of integration and were generally supportive of both its aims and mechanisms. Consequently, Ireland could be expected to enter negotiations on the next stage of integration with a positive approach, although with a different policy orientation on security matters to that of the other member states. This interpretation would be consistent with the intention to hold a further Inter Governmental Conference in 1996 on deepening the integration process and it would be understood that its conclusions would require a further referendum in this country.

Other member states would interpret the outcome as confirmation of Ireland's commitment to the European ideal and would respond accordingly. Ratification would furthermore have the benefit from a Community viewpoint of having a positive influence on public opinion in the applicant states, seeing that they would be expected to have some affinity with Ireland as a small neutral country.

The problem of interpretation would be of a different order in respect of a negative vote. Within Ireland, it could mean a number of

151

different things whereas within the rest of the Community it would probably lead to the single conclusion that Ireland had decided to opt out of the integration process. These differences could create major problems in determining the exact nature of Ireland's future relationship with the Union.

For example, the Irish interpretation of the rejection of the Treaty could consist of any one of three viewpoints which are mutually contradictory. These range from a policy of preventing the process of integration proceeding any further to one of negotiating Treaty amendments and, finally, to arranging Irish disengagement from the Community. It would be difficult to forecast which of the three viewpoints would be taken by the Irish government as expressing the democratic will of the people but it is easier to anticipate which is likely to be chosen by the other governments.

A negative vote, whatever the motivations behind it, is more likely to be interpreted by the other member states as a decision to opt out of the integration process rather than to stall or amend it. It would be held that they had negotiated in good faith with the Irish government and had accommodated its demands within the provisions of the Treaty but, notwithstanding all that, Ireland had rejected Maastricht. Common sense would suggest that the reaction of the other member state governments would be hostile, since the Treaty can not come into force unless all twelve High Contracting Parties ratify it in accordance with their constitutional requirements. A failure to ratify would frustrate the intention to create EMU, establish a common foreign and security policy and extend the policy competence of the European Community, to mention just three of the major casualties. Hence, the most likely interpretation on their part would be that Ireland had judged these key developments to be unacceptable and could proceed no further with unification. This difference in interpretation of the outcome could have major institutional implications for Ireland's future relationship with any new Union.

Implications

The implication of a positive vote can be briefly summarised. The obligations of membership of the Union would be confined to the Treaty provisions. As a participant in the process towards EMU, Ireland would benefit from the Delors II package in whatever form is finally agreed. By contrast,the legal and constitutional implications of a negative vote are more difficult to predict. Much would depend on the political goodwill of the other member states. At best, in the event of the Union proceeding, Ireland could develop an association with it but the institutional form of any association is impossible to forecast with certainty since it could range from quasi-membership to virtual expulsion.

However, the immediate reaction to a negative vote would be more political than legal since that is the essential nature of the integration process which must be understood in terms of dynamic politics rather than precise legalisms. The theoretical possibility of reconvening an Inter Governmental Conference and opening negotiations (on whatever the Irish government would regard as the reasons provoking a no vote) might be quickly dismissed if the other member states remained determined to press on with further integration.

The famous Pandora's box would be kept firmly closed for the reason that to open it for one member state would incite pressure within others to have the same facility. An amended Treaty, simply taking account of the special requirements of one member state would have to go through the ratification process of all the member states and would be open to the understandable popular objection that the Irish government had been able to do what other governments had failed to accomplish. The renegotiation strategy would seem to carry little credibility in political terms.

If the political will existed, and the stress is necessarily on the expression of this conditionality, then the other member states, interpreting a negative vote as a decision by Ireland to opt out of the unification process, could decide for themselves to proceed as planned at Maastricht by re-adopting its provisions as they stand (except for excising all references to Ireland). It has been argued that such a scenario is impossible because Maastricht builds on the foundations of the existing Treaties and *acquis communautaire* and consequently Ireland could prevent the other eleven member states going ahead since it requires the assent of all twelve to amend the Treaties. Legally, this is a correct interpretation but politically it ignores the fact that the other states are free to do whatever they wish.

For example, one mechanism would be to leave the existing Community stand as a legal structure but allow it to wither politically. The new European Union could be established *de novo* on some fixed date and could incorporate the existing Treaties and entire *acquis communautaire*. However, Irish opposition to using the existing Treaties and institutions for proceeding to European Union is unlikely as it would be a political act which could only expect a political riposte. It would hardly be restrained. More likely, the Irish government would accept the verdict of the people that Maastricht was unacceptable, admit to the impossibility of renegotiating elements of the Treaty, acquiesce to the other member states proceeding as they wish towards European union and attempt to establish some form of association with whatever new Union emerges. A negative vote would therefore be reduced to only one of the three strategies believed possible before the referendum – that of association.

This strategy would not be without difficulties. Chapter 13 has analysed the legal consequences of a non-ratification and the possibility of a two-tiered membership of the Community. The opinion offered is to the effect that the majority of new legislation would not be applicable to and in Ireland if a two-tiered Community (or Union) were established and that Ireland would very quickly become a member in name only. It goes further by stating that the European Court of Justice might find two-tiered membership to be incompatible with the EC Treaty itself, deeming it to conflict with the very foundations of the Community. If that proved to be the case, there could be no acceptable amendment to the Treaty which would make two-tiered membership possible.

This suggests that there could be insurmountable obstacles within the Treaties regarding a system of two-tiered membership, which some have advocated as a viable alternative to adopting Maastricht. It is always possible, of course, that the Court of Justice would find differently but the chances of that happening must be regarded as doubtful. It would be extremely unwise to predicate a future strategy for this country on the grounds that a two-tiered membership is both legally and politically possible. All the evidence points the other way.

If European Union goes ahead despite our failure to ratify Maastricht, then the implications of a no vote can at best be presented as implying a place in a second tier of the new Union and, at worst, as opting out altogether in favour of an unspecified association. If the Union does not go ahead because of a crisis precipitated by our non-ratification, then the main implication is that there would be a heavy price to pay politically in terms of goodwill and economically in terms of the stagnation of the existing Community.

Economic Consequences

The economic consequences of the ratification of Maastricht can be more confidently predicted than those flowing from its rejection. The reason is that the framework of existing EC policies is known, future policies can be predicted on the basis of the Treaty's provisions, some broad estimates can be made of increased EC transfers and the general thrust of national development programmes could be expected to continue. If Ireland enters the European Union, then the degree of interdependence with other member state economies will intensify. All these factors constitute a scenario for the medium term which can be evaluated with reasonable certainty.

On the other hand, a negative vote would immediately introduce major uncertainties which would change the existing policy framework. One consequence is that, irrespective of the different reasons which might have led to the rejection of Maastricht, it is virtually certain that the business community at home and elsewhere would interpret it as a decision to opt out of the integration process. Their expectations as to the future would be turned upside down and the first casualty would be business confidence itself, which has such a decisive bearing on the performance of the markets and long-term investment strategies.

There would be few economists who would deny that the immediate impact would be on the money markets where the lack of confidence would have to be compensated by an increase in interest rates in order to stem capital outflows and defend the value of the currency. The knock-on effect on business costs are predictable. Similarly, the public finances would be adversely affected through a rise in debt servicing and it would have to be anticipated that the budgetary situation would be further worsened through some losses of EC transfers. Other short-term effects would include the likely negative reaction of the stock exchange and, at the very least, postponement of pending investment decisions.

Even if our economic relationship with Europe was regularised in some fashion in the medium term, the impact on growth could be severe. Ireland's participation in the Community and in EMU has been taken for granted by the business community and strategies have been formulated accordingly. The reversal of this basic planning assumption would inevitably put many projects in doubt and the attractiveness of the country as an investment location would be greatly lessened. The loss of elements of the Structural Funds would slow down the modernisation of the infrastructure and would have long-term implications for competitiveness.

The impact on international trade is more difficult to forecast but the effect on exports could be serious given that the Single Market will be the dominating influence in cross border business relationships and networking. The outcome for agriculture would obviously depend on whatever relationship could be maintained with the CAP but it could hardly be expected to be equivalent to full membership. All in all, the medium-term prospects for economic growth would be poorer, with obvious consequences for employment and living standards.

The above scenario is one possible outcome of a negative vote. Clearly there could be others if, for example, a two-tiered membership of the Union could be achieved or if the Union itself did not go ahead as a direct result of Ireland's rejection of the Treaty. But either of these two possibilities contain elements similar to those outlined above and could not be anything but negative to some extent. In the end, the economic consequences of a no vote range from those associated with some undefined form of external relationship with the European Union, membership within a second tier or continued participation within a politically weakened Community.

As against these scenarios it has been argued that the Irish economy could develop on the basis of its own resources and intellectual abilities. A development strategy could be independently determined in the context of bi-lateral relations with other countries and a favoured relationship with the European Community or new Union. This may be attractive as another version of the appeal to independence but it would hardly correspond with the realities of global markets which have led other states to conclude that their economic future lies inside rather than outside a single European economy.

Protocol 17

The previous chapter analysing the issues raised by the Treaty on European Union did not advert to Protocol 17 as, strictly speaking, it relates to Irish public policy rather than to the objectives and mechanisms of the integration process. There is. of course, an inter-relationship between the effect of Article 40.3.3 of the Constitution and certain rights arising from the Treaties which have become the subject of public controversy. That relationship was analysed legally in Chapter 14. In terms of the political options facing the electorate in the referendum, it is appropriate to comment on that inter-relationship from the different perspective of analysing European integration as a dynamic political process.

In that context, one feature of European unification needs to be restressed. Public morality and the manner of its expression either in national constitutions or legal systems is solely a matter for the member states themselves within their jurisdictions. The intent of Protocol 17 was to give expression to that reality by protecting the effect of Article 40.3.3 within Ireland as it was understood at the time of signing the Treaty at Maastricht. It subsequently transpired as a result of the Constitutional actions analysed in Chapter 14, that the amendment had other unanticipated effects and the Government decided to take them into account by introducing additional amendments later this year. This raised the issue of the relationship between the Protocol as it stands and any future amendments which may be made to Article 40.3.3. The matter has been considered in a Solemn Declaration on behalf of the High Contracting Parties to the Treaty. It states, *inter alia*, that if Ireland so requests they are willing to extend the scope of the Protocol to these constitutional amendments.

Legal interpretation of the Declaration in so far as it affects the current wording of the Protocol properly belongs to the province of law. But in respect of its future effect it must also be assessed within the larger context in which integration actually proceeds as a *political process*. Otherwise the interpretation as it affects the referendum will be too narrow. A Solemn Declaration is a statement of political will by the governments of member states in which they commit themselves to a course of action and is open to no other interpretation in the context of integration except as a commitment to act. In this case, the action is to be undertaken, on the one hand, by Ireland and, on the other, by all of the High Contracting Parties acting collegially, including Ireland.

A political commitment to future action in the legislative sphere is a commonplace feature of the various Councils of Ministers but when underwritten, as in this instance, with the solemnity of the member states acting as High Contracting Parties, it is elevated to a special status which goes beyond the norm. As such it can be understood to mean that if Ireland should amend its constitution, then any necessary consequential amendment to the Protocol will be made by the signatories to the Treaty.

This interpretation of the Solemn Declaration goes beyond the narrower confines of the law by taking into account the reality that the process of European integration is a political process in which law evolves dynamically and follows the political intent of the member states. It is this fact, one which can be verified from the actual experience of integration, which amplifies the legal designation of the Solemn Declaration as a "hollow instrument" and permits the conclusion that instead it will be the instrument for whatever legislative action may be deemed necessary by the Irish people in the first instance and by the High Contracting Parties as a direct consequence.

Present Choices And Future Strategies

The two basic choices facing the electorate have emerged as a compendium of intentions, interpretations, implications and consequences but in the end will come down to a decision on the preferred option for this country's future relationship with the European Union and, as stated at the outset, that is ultimately a political choice as to where our destiny should lie. The policy options facing us as a people can be summarised in terms of the following political strategies.

The ratification of Maastricht can be presented as a decision to remain within the process of European unification but on the basis of separately judging each step as it arises. This strategy would accept the Monnet method as the mechanism for deepening and widening integration. It would be clearly understood that Ireland, like the other member states, retains the right to protect its vital national interests while being simultaneously committed to greater interdependence within the framework of the European Union. Such a strategy could be termed *conditional commitment* and would imply that Ireland would play a proactive role in shaping the Union on the basis of clear cut ideas and policies.

The ratification could also be presented as the *passive acceptance* of the unification process in which economic benefits were deemed to outweigh any sacrifices of political independence. This option is close to the one pursued to date but will be untenable at some point, most likely at the next stage of integration in 1996.

Theoretically, the endorsement of Maastricht could be regarded as an *unquestioning* acceptance of the goal of unification and a general willingness to comply with each stage of the process. This is sometimes put forward as the policy of those who call themselves federalists but unconditional commitment has little relevance in the political life of this country.

The rejection of the Treaty involves a number of options depending on the degree to which some association with 'Europe' is considered desirable.

One strategy favours the *maintenance of the status quo* in the belief that any member state can frustrate the move to European Union by refusing to ratify the Treaty. Its credibility depends on two factors, the political will of the other member states to proceed without Ireland or the capacity of the Community to hold together should non-ratification throw it into crisis.

The second is that of *renegotiation* and this presumes another IGC would be convened in which Ireland works out either a series of special derogations in relation to EMU or the CFSP (or both) or else that these key elements are somehow amended for all member states. Obviously this depends on the willingness of the other member states to engage in renegotiation on the same basis as the first negotiation.

The third strategy based on non-ratification could be styled as one of *association* either within a second tier of membership or through an external relationship. Either way, this strategy can be termed as *conscious opting out* of the European project.

There are other possible variations on the theme of saying no to Maastricht but the conclusion of Chapter 14 is that they would in all probability have the same end result. Ireland would limit or end its involvement in the programme of unification and with the passage of time any limited form of association could deteriorate into non-membership.

In concrete political terms two strategic options stand out. On the one hand, the ratification of the Treaty as a form of conditional commitment to European unification and on the other, non-ratification as a means of ending that commitment and substituting external association in its place. These are the two real choices posed by Maastricht. The response by the electorate to these alternate and contradictory visions of ourselves and of Europe will be the most important political decision of this generation.

SUMMARY

Part One: The Context

CHAPTER 1. FROM COMMUNITY TO UNION

The term 'union' lacks precision. It has been used to refer to involuntary unions (the Act of Union, the Soviet Union), but in this case we are concerned with a treaty-based association of more or less autonomous but interdependent states. This form of Union is broadly confederal with several antecedents in European history, usually motivated by considerations of security or economic welfare. Both motives were significant in the development of integration in Western Europe after World War II. The European Community was seen not just as 'an economic and social undertaking'; it was to create "a continent which is economically and politically united". During Ireland's membership of the EC the latter goal has often seemed remote. However, the revival of integration in the mid-1980s, and the dramatic changes in world politics since 1989, have combined to create demands for a more ambitious approach. The Treaty on European Union, negotiated throughout 1991, represents the culmination of these forces.

The most ambitious model of integration is the transformation of the existing confederation into a single federal state. By identifying the policies and institutions of the federal model we can establish a measure of how far the Treaty of Maastricht has moved in this direction. It is suggested that it has not yet advanced to the threshold of a federal union, but is still best understood as a very complex confederation.

160

Part Two: The Union Processes

CHAPTER 2. THE TREATY: STRUCTURE AND THEMES

The Treaty of Maastricht defines European Union as consisting of three pillars, namely, amendments to the EEC Treaties (including the provision on Economic and Monetary Union), provisions on a Common Foreign and Security policy, and provisions on Judicial Cooperation and Home Affairs. This structure incorporates two distinct decision-making frameworks. The supranational Community method dominates the European Community pillar whereas the other two are characterised by less constraining intergovernmental arrangements. 'Subsidiarity' has emerged as a guiding principle in the Treaty. This means that the Union should only engage in activities if particular policy problems cannot be solved by a lower tier of government.

CHAPTER 3. THE NEW INSTITUTIONAL FRAMEWORK

Institutional change has been an important feature of the Community's development. The Treaty of Maastricht includes a number of changes to the role and functions of the institutions. The European Council emerges as the centre of political authority in the Union. Provision is made for a greater use of qualified majority in the Council. The Parliament is granted a limited form of co-decision with the Council, its assent powers have been extended and it must now vote on the appointment of the Commission. The Treaty of Maastricht has done little to reduce the complexity of the Community's decision-making system. The three pillars lead to different policy frameworks in which the role of individual institutions differs one from the other. There are now more complicated decision-making rules both in the Council and between the Council and the Parliament.

CHAPTER 4. HOW DEMOCRATIC IS THE UNION?

If the complexity of the Union's decision-making rules makes it difficult to predict their effectiveness, the same may be said for the 'transparency' and, therefore, the accountability of the new processes. The European Parliament's position in the institutional balance has been strengthened, but its new powers are offset to some extent by the Council's greater use of majority voting and the fragmented structure of the Treaty. However, the role of national parliaments has received little attention, though this may be remedied at the national level. A new Committee of the Regions has some potential for developing as an additional arena for democratic representation though its powers are negligible. For the first time citizenship of the Union is defined, in terms of rights of residence, movement and political participation. Consumer protection and access to a European Ombudsman are also included, though the cumulative rulings of the European Court of Justice and the incorporation of the European Convention on Human Rights remain the best safeguards of the citizens' rights.

Part Three: The Community Pillar

CHAPTER 5. NEW POLICIES

The policy scope of the Union is built on the existing treaties but also represents a major extension of the role of the Union, notably in relation to EMU. Policy issues that find a place in the new Treaty include culture, education, development co-operation, health, and trans-European networks. Subsidiarity will govern the boundaries of the Community's role in these fields.

CHAPTER 6. ECONOMIC AND MONETARY UNION

Economic and Monetary Union (EMU) is now significant for three reasons: as an important step in the completion of the Single Market; as an attempt to secure a macroeconomic environment of low inflation and steady growth; and as a significant step towards political union. The new Treaty outlines economic objectives, policy instruments, rules governing national economic policy and a timetable for transition to EMU. However, the actual system of monetary and economic management which emerges will be determined in the processes of European politics, at both national and Community level. The Treaty reflects the preoccupation with inflation which has dominated European politics and economic policy for the last decade and a half. To assuage German fears about losing the Deutschmark, the system, at least on paper, gives higher priority to price stability than either the German or US systems.

Although the Treaty lays down rules for the size of national debt and budget deficits, these are likely to be interpreted in a flexible way. There is some provision for increased coordination of national economic policies. A central question is whether the set of Community economic policies will be sufficient to pursue Community goals other than price stability – especially employment, growth and cohesion. Two questions are particularly important for Ireland. First, does EMU offer the prospect of a better macroeconomic performance than the alternatives of EMS or a floating currency ? Second, what is the likely regional pattern of economic activity and income in EMU ?

CHAPTER 7. COHESION

The term 'economic and social cohesion' refers to the goal of reducing the amount of social and regional inequality between countries, regions and social groups. The Treaty of Maastricht contains significant additional references to cohesion, but cohesion policies are only one of many factors which shape the regional pattern of economic activity and income in Europe.

The Commission is to submit a report every three years on progress made towards economic and social cohesion. While the Structural Funds will continue to play a major role they are to be reviewed and modified. A new Cohesion Fund is to be established to provide support for projects in the fields of environment and trans-European networks in the area of infrastructure. There is also the intention to modify the Community's system of 'own resources' or taxation. The current system is regressive in that poorer member states can pay proportionately more than richer ones.

Cohesion policy is primarily a matter for the political process in the Community rather than one which can be dealt with in binding Treaty provisions. Consequently, from an Irish perspective, the forthcoming review of the Structural Funds and the establishment of a new Community financial perspective and budget are at least as significant as the provisions of the Treaty of Maastricht.

Since the Treaty ensures that the cohesion issue remains permanently on the Community agenda, it opens the possibility that, at some stage, experience or argument will prompt the development of new approaches and/or very much more substantial cohesion policies.

CHAPTER 8. SOCIAL POLICY

Social Policy, meaning in the EC context policy in respect of workers' rights and welfare, caused a major problem in Maastricht. The Draft Treaty envisaged more extensive powers for the EC, but the United Kingdom baulked at this. A new EC solution to an EC problem was devised. The twelve member states agreed in a Protocol that this section of the Treaty, now an Agreement on Social policy, would apply to, and be implemented by, the eleven, excluding the United Kingdom. On the face of it this could give the UK the advantage of lower labour costs; in the event, given other integrating dynamics in the European economy, the advantage is unlikely to be of any significance. In the Agreement, social policy objectives are considerably expanded and on many of them progress can be made by qualified majority voting; and the "social dialogue" at the EC level is given a new importance. There are also important social policy initiatives in the rest of the Treaty. The reform of the Structural Funds in general promises more scope for subventing national social programmes, and for the first time education and public health have been firmly on the EC agenda.

Part Four: The Intergovernmental Pillars

CHAPTER 9. COMMON FOREIGN AND SECURITY POLICY

So far as the Union's external action is concerned, the new provisions for a Common Foreign and Security Policy (CFSP) are the principal focus of attention. They form a separate pillar in the Treaty, with an intergovernmental legal base and a refinement of familiar procedures. However, the attempt to introduce a limited measure of majority voting into foreign policy, through the concept of 'joint action', does in principle represent a departure from the doctrine of external sovereignty. Yet it is remarkably circumscribed in legal terms, and it is unlikely that governments, especially the larger ones, will abandon their freedom of manoeuvre on a point of substance. The European Parliament's oversight of foreign policy is only marginally improved.

Although there is no commitment to military alliance in the Treaty, defence is on the medium-term horizon, being included as a future objective which will be the subject of another Inter Governmental Conference in the mid-1990s. Differences between 'Europeanist' and 'Atlanticist' views on defence have thus put off hard questions about Irish neutrality, though probably not for very long. The dominant role of the United States in European security can no longer be taken for granted, and new security challenges are leading to a fundamental reappraisal of security and defence policies.

Already the Treaty envisages the European Union 'contracting out' some security tasks to the Western European Union (WEU). The latter organisation, an embryonic military alliance, has a membership which overlaps both the EC and NATO. However, it will only be used by the European Union on the basis of a unanimous request. Ireland is not bound by the WEU's decisions, but the development of the WEU is likely to be a central element in the security of the new Europe. This may pose dilemmas for Irish governments during the next few years. It is in Ireland's interest to influence the direction of security policy; can this be done from outside the evolving system? The possibility of observer status, offered by the WEU at Maastricht, is relevant in this context.

CHAPTER 10. COOPERATION IN JUSTICE AND HOME AFFAIRS

The member states of the European Community began to cooperate on judicial matters in the 1970s outside the strict confines of the Treaties. This cooperation has now been codified in the Treaty of Maastricht as a separate pillar of the Union. Cooperation in this field is directed largely towards limiting serious crime and in establishing a framework for dealing with the free movement of people in the Single Market. Cooperation focuses particularly on the access of third country nationals to the Union and their rights within it.

Part Five: Europe After Maastricht

CHAPTER 11. ENLARGEMENT

Enlargement will be a central political challenge for the European Union in the decade ahead. It is now clear that an initial phase of expansion, involving Austria, Sweden and Finland, is likely within three or four years. This will be followed by countries such as Hungary, Czechoslovakia and Poland, while other applications, or statements of intention to apply, pile up.

Enlargement gives rise to controversy on the future size and shape of the European Union, and in particular on its degree of openness or exclusiveness. It further puts the spotlight on key policy areas - balanced economic and social development; the Community's Budget as an instrument of cohesion; the debate on security and defence and, above all, the need for institutional change to permit a Union of over twenty states to operate with efficiency while maintaining its drive towards integration.

For Ireland, the Enlargement issue necessitates a new debate on the fundamentals of European commitment, and on the very practical questions of economic competition, cohesion, neutrality, and the balance of power in the Union institutions.

CHAPTER 12. TOWARDS A FEDERAL UNION?

How does the Treaty as a whole measure up to the federal ambitions which have been an implicit part of European integration ? The policy content has expanded, as a mixture of quasi-federal elements, especially EMU, and other activities which fall short of that mark. The policy process is an increasingly complex hybrid of federal and intergovernmental ideas, raising important issues of efficiency and democratic accountability. Any assessment of Ireland's interests will thus have to balance the probable effects of policy changes against the even less tangible consequences of further losses of national sovereignty.

However, the Treaty neither creates a federal union nor does it approach the level of integration which could be regarded as the threshold of a federal Europe. The European Union is about changing an existing confederation into a higher gear. Whether it is high enough to face the many challenges on the European agenda, particularly that of a major enlargement, is doubtful. Hence a further reform of the Union has already been planned for the mid-1990s. This could lead to a more emphatic step in the federal direction, but the continuing uncertainties in world and European politics mean that this is only one of several scenarios for the medium term.

Part Six: The Treaty And The Constitution

CHAPTER 13. THE LEGAL AND CONSTITUTIONAL IMPLICATIONS

It is necessary to have a referendum due to the fact that the Treaty on European Union goes far beyond anything that the EC has hitherto attempted, resulting in a significant change in the nature and structure of the Community. Such a change could not be deemed to be "necessitated by the obligations of membership of the Communities" and therefore a referendum is required to give it constitutional protection.

The second issue examined is the legal consequences of non-ratification by Ireland of the Treaty. In that event the Treaty on European Union could not go ahead. However, it is possible that the other member states would attempt to devise a system of two-tiered membership whereby those member states who do not wish to be part of a European Union would remain in the existing Community and the remainder of the member states would sign a new Treaty, similar to the existing Treaty on European Union.

The consequences for Ireland should such a system of two-tiered membership come into effect are examined. It is likely that Ireland could neither participate in any legislative processes under the new system, nor would any legislation passed under the new system be applicable in Ireland. An analysis of the legality of a system of two-tiered membership also suggests that the creation of this type of system faces many legal obstacles no matter how it is approached. Finally, on the issue of future changes which might affect Ireland's neutrality, although the Treaty advances the cause of further European integration, it does not create a form of European Union which would lead to the disappearance of the individual nation states. The ultimate creation of a common defence policy and common defence structures within the Union will require a further Intergovernmental Conference followed by another referendum.

CHAPTER 14. PROTOCOL 17

The Protocol appears to have been designed to ensure that the abortion and Maastricht debates did not become inter-linked. It seems to have had the twin purposes of (a) guarding against the introduction of EC-sponsored abortion legislation and (b) protecting the information ban from any challenge based on Community law grounds. However, the decision in the X case has changed the entire background to the Protocol, especially since that decision (a) allows for abortion in limited cases and (b) sanctions the granting of travel injunctions in order to vindicate the provisions of Article 40.3.3 in cases where the abortion would not be lawful in this state.

The Protocol appears to have the effect of withdrawing the application of EC law in abortion cases "in Ireland" within the meaning of the Protocol. The meaning "in Ireland" is apt to give rise to difficulties, but it seems that were the facts of the X case to be repeated, the granting of the travel injunction would have represented the "application in Ireland of Article 40.3.3 of the Constitution of Ireland", so that no reliance could be placed on the application of EC law in that context.

A further difficulty is that another consequence of the Protocol might be to "freeze" the existing Article 40.3.3. In other words, the protection given is to the existing constitutional provision, so that any version of Article 40.3.3 would not enjoy the requisite degree of protection at EC level. The promise contained in the Solemn Declaration to consider changing the Protocol in the wake of such constitutional change is a useful indicator of future political intent; however, the Declaration, insofar as it purports to interpret the Protocol has no legal standing and cannot be relied on for this purpose.

Part Seven: Ireland And The Union

CHAPTER 15. ISSUES

The central question in the referendum is whether the Irish people wish to be part of an enterprise which might in time lead to political as well as economic unity among the peoples of Europe. European Union could be said to mark the end of the first phase of the integration process and the start of a new phase when the ultimate goal of unification merits serious debate. The perennial question of political identity and allegiance is raised in a new form: are we not just Irish but European as well?

The political meaning of 'Europe' has been associated with a process of integration which by the end of the century will have been underway for fifty years, and which will have spread from six to about twenty member states. Involvement in this process involves sharing elements of sovereignty. In previous referendums in 1972 and 1987, the electorate accepted limitations in economic sovereignty, thus endorsing the widely held view that no national economy in Europe can be independently managed. However, the question of sharing political sovereignty implies a tension between the role of the nation state and European unity.

The Maastricht Treaty proposes a balance between the competing demands of separateness and mutual dependence. The proposition that it establishes an embryonic superstate which will impose a homogenous value system over twenty or more long-established nation states ignores both this diversity and the diffuse system of government the Treaty entails. The autonomy of the national constitution and system of laws is preserved.

The aim to move towards a common defence policy raises the issue of neutrality, a potent symbol of Ireland's independence. By the time that issue has to be resolved, in 1996, the values of neutrality will have to be taken as the policy principles of a significant minority of the actual Union membership, and not just Ireland. The objectives of preserving peace and agreeing a common security system for Europe pose a vital challenge for the post-Maastricht period, and any departure from neutrality would necessitate a further referendum.

Another fundamental issue which was not resolved at Maastricht was whether a united Europe should be federal in character. The preference for a diffused system of political authority may not be easy to reconcile with the need for a cohesive political centre with the capacity to redistribute resources to less favoured regions.

The economic focus of the Treaty is the commitment to Economic and Monetary Union. Membership of the final stage of EMU is likely to be, if anything, less onerous than involvement in the EMS. The interim stages may be more problematic. They require a year on year reduction in the national debt, but fears that this would be excessively deflationary should be put in the context of the existing national consensus that the level of debt must be reduced.

The tendency of the core to benefit at the expense of peripheral regions is compensated in principle by Cohesion policy. The capacity of a monetary union covering twelve economies is at stake, and the importance of regional aid has grown proportionately to the scale of integration. The size and allocation of the Cohesion Funds remain an issue for negotiation.

The key requirement is to improve competitiveness on a constant basis. Every national economy is affected by the globalisation of markets, imposing a stark choice between membership of EMU, with the negative effects being tempered by cohesion, or an external association with it, relying on our own resources to deal with the same effects. For two decades Irish development policy has been based on EC membership, and the continuation of that policy should be a central issue in the referendum debate.

CHAPTER 16. OPTIONS

The choice in the referendum will reflect the electorate's intentions towards Ireland's future in Europe. A positive vote will be interpreted as a democratic validation of the changes made in the Maastricht Treaty, and the implications of such a decision can be assessed in terms of those changes.

A negative vote may be open to a variety of interpretations, ranging from a wish to freeze Ireland's involvement in integration to a decision to disengage. The implications of this outcome are more difficult to predict, though the increased level of uncertainty it would cause would probably result in major negative economic consequences in the short term. Medium to long term implications are also problematic, especially given the difficulties inherent in devising and operating a two-tier system of membership.

Several strategic options are considered, but, in concrete political terms, two stand out. Ratification of the Treaty is a form of conditional commitment to European unification; on the other hand, non-ratification is a means of ending that commitment and substituting external association for it. The choice made by the electorate will be the most important political decision of this generation.

LIST OF ABBREVIATIONS

CAP	Common Agricultural Policy
CEEP	European Centre of Public Enterprise
CFSP	Common Foreign and Security Policy
CIS	Commonwealth of Independent States
CSCE	Conference on Security and Cooperation in Europe
EC	European Community
ECB	European Central Bank
ECHR	European Convention on Human Rights
ECJ	European Court of Justice
ECSC	European Coal and Steel Community
ECU	European Currency Unit (ecu)
EEA	European Economic Area
EEC	European Economic Community
EFTA	European Free Trade Association
EMI	European Monetary Institute
EMS	European Monetary System
EMU	Economic and Monetary Union
EP	European Parliament
EPC	European Political Cooperation
ESCB	European System of Central Banks
ESF	European Social Fund
ETUC	European Trade Union Congress

EURATOM	European Atomic Energy Community
EUROPOL	European Central Criminal Investigation Office
GATT	General Agreement on Tariffs and Trade
GDP	Gross Domestic Product
GNP	Gross National Product
IGC	Inter Governmental Conference
MEP	Member of the European Parliament
NACC	North Atlantic Cooperation Council
NATO	North Atlantic Treaty Organisation
NESC	The National Economic and Social Council
SEA	Single European Act
TREVI	Terrorism, Radicalism, Extremism, Violence International (Consultation procedure among EC Ministers of the Interior or Justice)
UN	United Nations
UNICE	Union of European Employers Organisations
WEU	Western European Union

AUTHORS' BIOGRAPHIES

James Dooge is a civil engineer and hydrologist. He has been President of the Institution of Engineers in Ireland, the Royal Irish Academy, and the International Association for Hydrologic Sciences. He is the current President-Elect of the International Council of Scientific Unions. His political career began when he was elected to Seanad Eireann in 1961, and he was Leas Cathaoirleach from 1965-73, Cathaoirleach from 1973-77, and Leader of the Seanad from 1983-87. In 1981-82 he was Minister for Foreign Affairs, and in 1984-85 was Chairman of the *ad hoc* Committee of personal representatives of EEC Heads of Government on Institutional Reform and European Union. He has subsequently been involved in EC evaluation of environmental research, and the impact of research and development on policy formation.

Tony Brown is an economist and European Affairs consultant, and a graduate of University College, Dublin. A Council Member of the Institute of European Affairs, he is Visiting Lecturer on European Institutions at St. Patrick's College, Maynooth. He has been active in EC industrial affairs, social policy and political bodies since the mid-1960s. He was a member of the Royal Irish Academy Committee on International Affairs from 1980-85, and is an Executive Member of the Irish Council of the European Movement. Since 1978 he has been International Secretary of the Labour Party and Council Member of the Socialist International.

Brendan Halligan is Chairperson of the Institute of European Affairs, managing partner of Consultants in Public Affairs, chairman of Bord na Móna, Chairperson of the Labour Party's International Affairs Committee and is a Council member of the Irish Council of the European Movement of which he is a former chairperson. He is a graduate of University College, Dublin and is presently Adjunct Professor of European Affairs in the University of Limerick. He held the position of General Secretary of the Labour Party from 1967 to 1980 and has been a member of the Dáil and Seanad Eireann and the European Parliament. He was treasurer of the Confederation of Socialist Parties in the European Communities for 1986 and 1988.

Gerard Hogan is a lecturer in Law at Trinity College, Dublin, and is a Barrister. A graduate of University College, Dublin, he is co-author of the Supplement to the second edition of Kelly's *The Irish Constitution* (1987) and *Political Violence and the Law in Ireland* (1989). He has written many articles, including 'The Supreme Court and the Single European Act', Irish Jurist, 22 (1987).

Niamh Hyland studied law at Trinity College, Dublin, where she became a Foundation Scholar in 1987. She graduated from Trinity in 1989 and then did a Master's degree in law at Magdalen College, Oxford. Between 1990-1991 she was a stagiaire in the Legal Service of the European Commission in the Social Affairs division. In 1991 she became Jean Monnet lecturer in European Law at Trinity College, Dublin.

Patrick Keatinge, Ph.D., is Associate Professor in Political Science at Trinity College, Dublin, where he teaches international politics. He is a graduate of TCD and the London School of Economics and Political Science. His publications include *The Formulation of Irish Foreign Policy* (1974), *A Place Among the Nations: Issues of Irish Foreign Policy* (1978), *A Singular Stance: Irish Neutrality in the 1980s* (1984), and many articles on Irish foreign policy. He recently edited *Ireland and EC Membership Evaluated* (1991).

Brigid Laffan, Ph.D., is Jean Monnet Professor in European Politics at University College, Dublin. She is a graduate of the University of Limerick, and the College of Europe in Bruges. She is author of numerous articles on European integration and has contributed to *Making European Policy Work* [H. Siedentopf and J. Ziller (eds.), 1988], *Ireland and EC Membership Evaluated* [P. Keatinge (ed.), 1991]. She wrote a book on *Ireland and South Africa: Government Policy in the 1980s* (1988), and her text on *Cooperation and Integration in Europe* will be published soon by Routledge.

Edward Moxon-Browne is Jean Monnet Professor in European Integration at the University of Limerick. He was educated at the Universities of St. Andrews and Pennsylvania and was Reader in Politics at Queen's University Belfast, to December, 1992. His main research interests are the European Parliament, Spanish membership of the European Community, the Community's peripheral regions, Irish politics, and the ethnic roots of political violence. Among his publications are *Nation, Class and Creed in Northern Ireland* (1983), *Political Change in Spain* (1989) and a monograph for the Irish Council of the European Movement entitled 'Relations Between the Oireachtas and Irish Members of the European Parliament after Direct Elections' (1979). He is currently writing a book on Spain's membership of the European Community.

Séamus Ó Cinnéide is a senior lecturer in Social Studies at St. Patrick's College, Maynooth, where he directs the Masters in European Social Policy Analysis. He is a graduate of the National University of Ireland and was called to the Bar in 1980. Since his 1970 book *A Law for the Poor,* he has written extensively on poverty, child care and juvenile justice, community development and social policy generally. He is a member of the central management group of the third EC poverty programme, Poverty 3, with responsibility for the evaluation of the programme. He is editing a report on Social Europe to be published by the IEA.

Rory O'Donnell is a Senior Research Officer at the Economic and Social Research Institute, Dublin. He was previously economist at Ireland's National Economic and Social Council, where he prepared the Council's report *Ireland in the European Community: Performance, Prospects and Strategy* (1989). His publications include *Adam Smith's Theory of Value and Distribution* (1990) and articles on the economics of European integration. He received his Ph.D. in economics from the University of Cambridge and has taught there and at University College, Dublin and University College, Galway.